11+
Non-verbal Reasoning

Multiple-choice Test Papers
Pack 1
The secrets of 11+ success

OXFORD
UNIVERSITY PRESS

Great Clarendon Street, Oxford, OX2 6DP, United Kingdom

Oxford University Press is a department of the University of Oxford. It furthers the University's objective of excellence in research, scholarship, and education by publishing worldwide. Oxford is a registered trade mark of Oxford University Press in the UK and in certain other countries

Text © Andrew Baines 2015
Illustrations © Oxford University Press 2015

The moral rights of the authors have been asserted

First published in 2015

All rights reserved. No part of this publication may be reproduced, stored in a retrieval system, or transmitted, in any form or by any means, without the prior permission in writing of Oxford University Press, or as expressly permitted by law, by licence or under terms agreed with the appropriate reprographics rights organization. Enquiries concerning reproduction outside the scope of the above should be sent to the Rights Department, Oxford University Press, at the address above.

You must not circulate this work in any other form and you must impose this same condition on any acquirer

British Library Cataloguing in Publication Data
Data available

978-0-19-274087-8

Paper used in the production of this book is a natural, recyclable product made from wood grown in sustainable forests. The manufacturing process conforms to the environmental regulations of the country of origin.

Printed in China

Acknowledgements

The publishers would like to thank the following for permissions to use copyright material:

Cover illustrations: Lo Cole

Although we have made every effort to trace and contact all copyright holders before publication this has not been possible in all cases. If notified, the publisher will rectify any errors or omissions at the earliest opportunity.

Links to third party websites are provided by Oxford in good faith and for information only. Oxford disclaims any responsibility for the materials contained in any third party website referenced in this work.

The manufacturer's authorised representative in the EU for product safety is Oxford University Press España S.A. of El Parque Empresarial San Fernando de Henares, Avenida de Castilla, 2 - 28830 Madrid (www.oup.es/en or product.safety@oup.com). OUP España S.A. also acts as importer into Spain of products made by the manufacturer.

The secrets of 11+ success in non-verbal reasoning

How 11+ exams work

Approaching 11+ exams for the first time can be a daunting experience. They are unlike any other school exam your child will take for several reasons:

- *There's no pass mark.* Success or failure depends on your child's performance relative to the performance of other children sitting the test. The pass mark can vary from year to year and from school to school.

- *They can't be retaken.* There is no second chance with the 11+ so it all rests on your child's performance on the day.

- *There's no national syllabus.* 11+ exams vary from area to area, and often from town to town. Often schools are extremely unwilling to give out any information about the content of the exams.

- *It's often impossible to see past papers.* This varies from area to area but the actual papers usually remain a closely guarded secret.

- *Selective schools give out very little advice.* It is common for selective schools to give out only the vaguest advice to parents when approaching the exam and to discourage very much practice.

All these factors make preparing a child for the 11+ a mysterious and often stressful process for parent and child alike. The most common question parents ask about using practice tests is 'What percentage does my child need to get to pass?' Unfortunately there's no easy answer to this but we can give guidance. (See 'What a score means and how to boost it' on page 4.) The second most common question is 'How can I help them improve?' The following sections give our tutors' top tips to help your child through the 11+ process and boost their scores. We strongly recommend that you think about purchasing at least two other essential Bond resources.

- *The Parents' Guide to the 11+.* The essential manual that provides a simple and practical 4-step system for making the most of 11+ preparation.

- *How To Do 11+ Non-verbal Reasoning.* All the question types in these tests are fully explained in this guide to 11+ non-verbal reasoning.

Tutors' top tips for 11+ success

- *Find out what exams your child will sit but don't agonise over 'school gate gossip'.* Find out what the exams are and get the advice that the secondary schools give out, but don't waste your energy following rumours about what the pass mark is or exactly which questions will come up. It's better to spend your time helping your child.

- *It's always worth practising.* Whatever secondary schools say, it's worth it. Children can improve their performance by 10–15 per cent by careful practice.

- *Start early if you can, but don't worry if you haven't.* Ideally it is best to start preparation for the 11+ exam at least one year ahead. However, don't panic if you don't have that much time; even a few weeks can make a difference.

- *Make a simple action plan.* However long you've got, have a clear, simple strategy. There are two key principles:
  - start from your child's present level of knowledge
  - help your child to learn from their mistakes.

  The Parents' Guide to the 11+ provides a set of ready-made action plans you can use, whether you have two years or just a few weeks to go.

- *Motivation, motivation, motivation!* You have to take your child with you on this journey. A simple rewards system can be highly effective. *The Parents' Guide to the 11+* can provide a tried and tested motivational system if you want one.

- *Don't just practise.* There's a tendency to think that just practising one paper after another will do the trick. It's far more important to learn from mistakes. Going through the paper afterwards with your child and filling in the gaps in learning is crucial.

- *Stay calm, manage stress, build confidence.* Don't talk about the 11+ all the time. Use breaks, treats and bite-sized learning sessions to keep things fresh. Be realistic about your child's potential. Pass or fail, it's important to try to make this process a positive one.

- *Manage the exam day.* Make sure that you have everything ready for the day, that your child tries to get a good night's sleep, eats breakfast and gets there in good time.

How and when to use these tests

- *It's best to use them as real exam practice.*
  These tests are mock exams. They are set out in a style as close as possible to the real thing – though the format will vary from area to area. It is best to use them as authentic exam experience quite close to the exams rather than for general practice, and to have practised non-verbal reasoning questions first, using Bond's Papers. Follow the instructions in the answers booklet on timings and administering the tests.

What's in a non-verbal reasoning exam?

Non-verbal reasoning is not a subject that your child will study as part of their school curriculum, but it is dependent on a set of core skills integral to maths, science, design and technology. It does not rely on literacy skills: all the questions are in pictorial or diagrammatic form.

The exact scope and content of an 11+ non-verbal reasoning test will differ across UK regions, but a typical paper will test your child's ability to:

- process graphic or pictorial information
- apply logical thinking and problem-solving skills
- understand how objects relate to each other in space (spatial awareness)
- find and follow patterns and rules
- apply maths skills: rotation, reflection and symmetry
- work systematically.

All non-verbal reasoning questions can be categorised into four main groups and a set of 10 question types. These papers practise most of the types; some, which are rarely set in 11+ exams, are not included here for lack of space, but are practised in the range of Bond Non-verbal Reasoning Assessment Papers. You will find a full explanation of all the non-verbal reasoning question types in *How To Do 11+ Non-verbal Reasoning*.

Group 1: Identifying shapes

1. Recognise shapes that are similar and different.
2. Identify shapes and patterns.
3. Pair up shapes.

These question types test understanding and recognition of shape and pattern. They rely on the ability to:

- find shapes that are similar or different
- sort given shapes or symbols according to their common features.

Group 2: Missing shapes

4. Find shapes that complete a sequence.
5. Find a given part within a shape.
6. Find a missing shape from a pattern.

These question types also test understanding of shape and pattern. They rely on the ability to:

- identify and apply a rule
- see shapes within shapes and patterns within patterns
- make deductions from given sets of objects or symbols.

Group 3: Rotating shapes

7. Recognise mirror images.
8. Link nets to cubes.

The principles of reflection and rotation of shapes form the basis of a range of non-verbal reasoning question types. These question types test:

- understanding of symmetry
- knowledge of 3-D shapes
- spatial awareness.

Group 4: Coded shapes and logic

9. Code and decode shapes.
10. Apply shape logic.

These question types test understanding of shape and logic skills. They rely on your ability to:

- think systematically and make deductions
- find and apply a given rule
- identify common features
- see shapes within shapes.

What a score means and how to boost it

For the reasons given above it is impossible to say that a certain score can guarantee a pass in the actual exams. However, we suggest that a score of 85% (51/60) would be a standard to aim at, without using this as a benchmark to frighten your child with. The best motivator is to see the scores going up. Here are some tried and tested tips for improvement:

- *Go over any incorrect answers.* Always go over incorrect answers so that your child can see what went wrong. To help with this process, each answer in these test papers is explained and also has an individual tutorial reference icon: [B3]. This icon links to the relevant section in *How To Do 11+ Non-verbal Reasoning* so your child can read more about the question type and complete more practice questions if needed.

- *Practise what you can't do.* Do all the practice you can at the questions you find hard.

- *Use the Next Steps Planner inside the back cover.* This will provide a plan for what to do next when a test has been marked.

- *Improve basic exam technique.* Work on improving speed, working efficiently – coming back to trickier questions later – and pacing over the 30 minutes.

- *Follow the golden rules above!*

Skills and games to help with non-verbal reasoning

In order to be successful at non-verbal reasoning there are a set of invaluable background skills to practise. These are the ability to:

- think logically
- analyse images
- spot common links, patterns, differences and rules
- relate objects to space
- work systematically.

1 *Reinforce key maths concepts.* A number of non-verbal reasoning question types are underpinned by some key maths skills, so it will be extremely beneficial to strengthen your child's understanding in these areas. In particular, your child needs to be comfortable working with:

- angles
- reflection
- lines of symmetry
- rotation
- 3-D shapes.

2 *Play games that develop non-verbal reasoning skills.* Playing games and solving puzzles are two of the best ways to improve observation and reasoning skills as well as to develop spatial awareness. Children are often more receptive to learning and developing skills when they don't realise that's what they're doing!

The following games and puzzles will prove helpful:

- Complete jigsaws and sliding-piece puzzles (complex pictures and numerous pieces will create more of a challenge).

- Work out 'spot the difference' puzzles (the more detail in an image, the greater the skills test).

- Decipher visual brainteasers – try one a day over breakfast.

- Play tiling games involving tetrominoes (e.g. Tetris) or pentominoes (e.g. Katamino). These types of puzzles are widely available for most games consoles and are often found on mobile phones. They promote spatial awareness and can also support your child's understanding of key maths concepts: rotation, symmetry, nets, area, perimeter and volume.

- Unravel other maths-based logic puzzles that can help to develop spatial awareness as well as strengthen basic maths abilities (e.g. Sudoku and Kakuro).

- Assemble 3-D interlocking or shape-building puzzles and construct 3-D modelling kits.

- Solve dissection puzzles such as tangrams. These Chinese puzzles encourage spatial awareness and problem-solving skills because they consist of seven geometric shapes that, when put together correctly, form a rectangle or a square. They can also be positioned in various outlines to form other shapes (e.g. an animal or a person). Ready-made tangram sets are widely available or you can have fun together making your own out of stiff card.

- Crack a Rubik's cube!

11+
Non-verbal Reasoning

Multiple-choice Test Papers
Pack 1
Notes and Answers

This booklet contains:

- advice on how to administer the tests
- answers
- tutors' explanations for every answer
- links to **How To Do 11+ Non-verbal Reasoning**

OXFORD
UNIVERSITY PRESS

Great Clarendon Street, Oxford, OX2 6DP, United Kingdom

Oxford University Press is a department of the University of Oxford. It furthers the University's objective of excellence in research, scholarship, and education by publishing worldwide. Oxford is a registered trade mark of Oxford University Press in the UK and in certain other countries

Text © Andrew Baines 2015
Illustrations © Oxford University Press 2015

The moral rights of the authors have been asserted

First published in 2015

All rights reserved. No part of this publication may be reproduced, stored in a retrieval system, or transmitted, in any form or by any means, without the prior permission in writing of Oxford University Press, or as expressly permitted by law, by licence or under terms agreed with the appropriate reprographics rights organization. Enquiries concerning reproduction outside the scope of the above should be sent to the Rights Department, Oxford University Press, at the address above.

You must not circulate this work in any other form and you must impose this same condition on any acquirer

British Library Cataloguing in Publication Data
Data available

978-0-19-274087-8

Paper used in the production of this book is a natural, recyclable product made from wood grown in sustainable forests. The manufacturing process conforms to the environmental regulations of the country of origin.

Printed in China

Acknowledgements

The publishers would like to thank the following for permissions to use copyright material:

Cover illustrations: Lo Cole

Although we have made every effort to trace and contact all copyright holders before publication this has not been possible in all cases. If notified, the publisher will rectify any errors or omissions at the earliest opportunity.

Links to third party websites are provided by Oxford in good faith and for information only. Oxford disclaims any responsibility for the materials contained in any third party website referenced in this work.

The manufacturer's authorised representative in the EU for product safety is Oxford University Press España S.A. of El Parque Empresarial San Fernando de Henares, Avenida de Castilla, 2 – 28830 Madrid (www.oup.es/en or product.safety@oup.com). OUP España S.A. also acts as importer into Spain of products made by the manufacturer.

How to administer the tests

What do you need?

- A quiet, well-lit place to sit the test.
- A stock of pencils. HB pencils are best for mulitple-choice papers.
- A pencil sharpener and an eraser.
- Blank paper for rough working.
- A clock or timer.

Before you start

Try to provide a calm yet formal atmosphere in which your child can take the test. It is important that you recreate the real test as closely as possible, so try to ensure your child has an appropriate work space and no distractions. Choose a time to do a test when your child is rested and relaxed.

Multiple-choice tests ask children to mark their answers in a separate answer booklet. Therefore, when reading the front page of the test paper with your child, point out the importance of answering carefully and rubbing out any altered answers clearly. (Read the section below for details of common pitfalls that can occur when using multiple-choice answer booklets.) Ensure that enough rough paper is available for working out answers; they should not use the empty space on the paper for workings.

Allow 30 minutes per test. On average, they will have just over 30 seconds to answer each question, so encourage them to move on from questions they are stuck on before too much time is wasted. Your child may find it helpful to put a cross in pencil by questions that have been missed out so that they can be quickly spotted later on. Remind them that they can always go back at the end if they have time left.

In order to provide an authentic test experience, this paper should be set in sections, as follows:

1. Go to Section 1 of the test booklet and work through the example with your child. Your child should then try the two practice questions; give them the correct answers when they have finished and discuss any difficulties with them. Explanations of how to do the practice questions are found in the 'Answers and explanations' section of this booklet. Your child should then complete Section 1. They have six minutes for this section. When the time is up they should stop writing. If they have not finished, draw a line at the point they have reached. You can always allow them to continue after the time to get more practice, or else leave the remaining questions for another time.

2. Proceed through the other sections in the same way.

If you do not wish to sit with your child through this process, adopt the following procedure:

1. Ask your child to work through the example and practice questions for all of the sections in the test booklet at their own speed. They should then look at the 'Answers and explanations' section of this booklet to ensure that they understand how to solve the practice questions for each section.

2. Tell your child to go back to Section 1 and begin the test questions. They should continue on to the next sections until they have finished all of the test questions in the test booklet, or until 30 minutes have passed. As there are five sections in the test booklet, inform your child that they will have six minutes for each section. When the time is up, if they have not finished all of the questions, they should draw a line at the point they have reached. They can always continue after the time to get more practice, or else leave the remaining questions for another time.

Encourage them to think about whether they should try to speed up, or to work more carefully, depending on how they finish the paper.

Using the multiple-choice answer booklet

If your child is sitting a multiple-choice exam it is crucial that they understand how to use the answer booklet properly. Spend time examining the booklet together. As you look through it explain that multiple-choice answer sheets are usually scored by computer rather than by hand (an optical reader scans the marks on each page). As a result, an answer will be classed as wrong if it is not clearly and accurately marked.

There are some common mistakes that are easy to make when using a multiple-choice answer booklet. Talk through the following points carefully with your child, without panicking them, but so that they understand exactly what they should/should not do:

- ***Marking outside the box.*** To record an answer, a clear line should be made through the centre of the relevant answer box. The line should stay within the border of the box so that it can be read accurately by the computer. To make sure your child knows how to mark each answer, show them how the sample answers are marked in the grey example boxes on the answer sheets in this pack.

- *Crossing out an answer.* If your child wants to change their mind they must never cross out an answer in a multiple-choice booklet. It must be fully rubbed out and then the new answer should be clearly marked in the appropriate box. If any mark is left in the first box, the computer could read two answers for that question and mark their response as incorrect.

- *Marking an answer in the wrong grid.* Answer grids often look the same on multiple-choice answer sheets so it is easy to mark an answer in the wrong grid, which can have a knock-on effect for all successive answers. Encourage your child to check that the question number of the grid matches the question they are answering before they make each mark. They should also take extra care if they decide to miss out a question to return to later.

- *Not pressing hard enough.* If a mark is too light, it may not be recognised by the computer and the question could be marked wrong. Remind your child that each answer needs to be marked clearly. We would suggest practising with soft HB pencils as they tend to make the clearest marks. If your child has to provide their own pencils for the actual test, make sure they take one or two HB pencils with them.

Marking and feedback

The answers that follow should be given one mark. Do not take marks away for wrong answers, but do not award half marks. You will end up with a score out of 60. Use the chart below as a guide for turning the score into a percentage. 51/60 equals the target score of 85% (see 'The secrets of 11+ success in non-verbal reasoning' booklet).

Marks	10	15	20	25	30	35	40	45	50	55
%	17	25	33	42	50	58	67	75	83	92

After marking, follow these steps:

- *Go over any incorrect answers.* Always go over incorrect answers so that your child can see what went wrong. To help with this process, each answer in these test papers is explained and also has an individual tutorial reference icon: B3. This icon links to the relevant section in *How To Do 11+ Non-verbal Reasoning* so your child can read more about the question type and complete more practice questions if needed.

- *Use the Next Steps Planner inside the back cover.* This will provide a plan for what to do next when a test has been marked.

Answers and explanations

Please refer to this diagram if you need help visualising the different angles that are referred to in some of the answer explanations below.

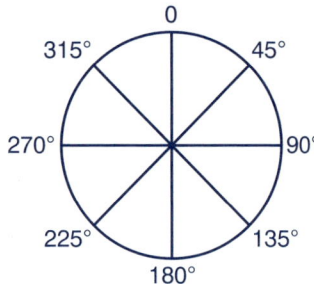

Test 1
Section 1

Practice 1
- e The shaded inner shape becomes unshaded and the unshaded inner shape becomes shaded.

Practice 2
- b The right-hand side of the shape becomes indented.
1. e The larger shape remains the same; however, the smaller outer shape is removed.
2. b The top halves of both shapes are removed.
3. a Step 1 The shape is rotated 90° anticlockwise.

      Step 2 The shape is copied, reflected horizontally (flipped over) and attached to the bottom.

      Step 3 The shading on the bottom half of the shape is reversed so that the shaded sections become clear and the clear sections become shaded.

      Step 4 The entire central square becomes unshaded.

4. a Step 1 The shape is rotated 90°.

      Step 2 A larger outline of the shape is added to the outside.

      Step 3 The hexagon is changed to a rectangle and sits only in the inner shape.

5. c Step 1 The size of the shape is reduced.
      Step 2 An identical shape is added to the left and shaded black.
6. d The solid outline of the shape is changed to a dotted line and a larger solid outine of the shape is added to the outside.
7. e Step 1 The shape is rotated 180°.
      Step 2 The solid lines in the centre of the shape are changed to dotted lines.
8. c Areas shaded black become unshaded and unshaded areas become striped.
9. a Step 1 The shape is reflected vertically (flipped to the right).

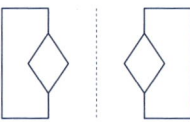

      Step 2 The solid lines that form the left-hand side of the shape and the central section are changed to dotted lines.
10. a The shape is rotated 180°.
11. b Step 1 The shape is repeated.
      Step 2 The inner shape is repeated and placed above the outer shape.
      Step 3 The inner shape becomes striped.
12. a The shape is rotated 90° clockwise and the areas with black shading become unshaded.

Section 2

Practice 1
- b The pattern is a hammer shape with no base and a rectangular head.

Practice 2
- d The inner shape is a square. The outer shape has one right angle (90°) and is a mixture of straight and curved lines.
1. b The total of all of the sides of the inner shapes is 10.
2. a The dotted line of symmetry divides the shape in half with the bottom half being the reflection (or mirror image) of the top half.
3. d Step 1 The inner shapes are a circle inside a rectangle, with the circle touching the sides of the rectangle.
      Step 2 The outer shape has four sides.
4. d The total of all of the sides of the inner shapes is 12.
5. a Both shapes are identical in size and shape.
6. a Each triangle has a small, a medium and a large version of the same shape. The smallest shape is unshaded and the medium and largest shapes are shaded.
7. b The shapes have horizontal lines of symmetry:

8. c The shape is made up of an unshaded right-angled triangle and a diagonally striped triangle that does not have a right angle.
9. d The composition of the shape is:
   - two boxes with crosses
   - one box shaded black
   - five unshaded boxes
   - four boxes with dots
   - four boxes with stripes
10. c Step 1 A small square is inside a larger square.
      Step 2 A circle is inside a pentagon.
      Step 3 The pentagon and larger square overlap.

11 **a** Step 1 A shape has a smaller version of the same shape inside.
Step 2 The shapes have four sides with a small square at each corner.
Step 3 The corner squares are positioned behind the larger shape.

12 **c** Step 1 The pattern inside the box (shown as a smiley face in the first shape) has a vertical line of symmetry.

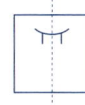

Step 2 The first horizontal line is in the same position in each box.
Step 3 The second horizontal line is in the same position and extends over the two vertical lines of the box border.

Section 3

Practice 1
  e The sequence is two pictures that alternate.

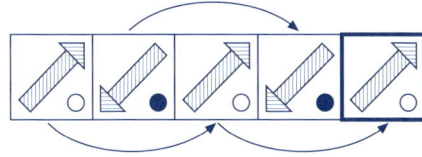

Practice 2
  a The number of stars and the number of solid straight edges increase by one each time.

1 **b** Step 1 The outer shape alternates between a pentagon and a square.
Step 2 The inner shape changes with each step in the sequence: each shape has one more side than the previous shape.

2 **b** Step 1 The number of small rectangles on the box borders is reduced by one each time.

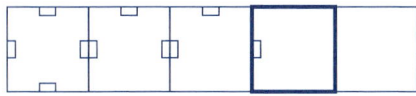

Step 2 The inner square loses one side in an anticlockwise direction each time.

Step 3 A line is added to the centre of the box each time in an anticlockwise direction. It eventually forms a cross.

Step 4 The number of corner points increases by one each time. These are added in an anticlockwise direction.

As it is the fourth in the sequence, the missing box must have one rectangle, one side of the square, three lines of the cross and three corner points:

3 **c** Step 1 A black square is added to a corner each time in an anticlockwise direction.

Step 2 The number of small black dots increases by one each time as they move around the edges of the shape in an anticlockwise direction.

The missing box must have two black squares and two dots on the sloping edge:

4 **a** This sequence has two alternating patterns. Each pattern follows the same rule.
Step 1 In the first pattern the contents of box 1 rotate 180° to form box 3. The contents of box 3 rotate 180° to form box 5.

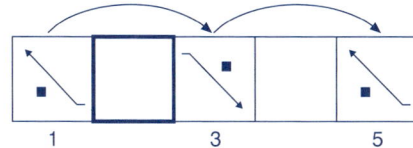

Step 2 In the second pattern box 4 must have been formed by the contents of box 2 being rotated 180°.

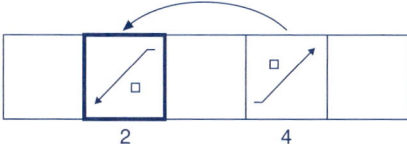

5 **b** Step 1 The arrow moves 135° in a clockwise direction.

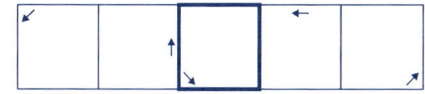

Step 2 The bottom trapezium (▲) is always shaded black.
Step 3 The central square alternates: boxes 1, 3 and 5 show the same shading and boxes 2 and 4 show the same shading.

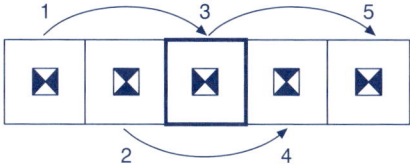

Step 4 The striped trapezium moves anticlockwise. When it reaches the bottom position it is hidden because this trapezium is always black (see Step 2).

Step 5 The small circle moves clockwise but when it reaches the bottom position it is hidden (see above).

The missing box must therefore look like this:

6 a Step 1 The number of black arrows starts at two, goes down one each time until zero, then the sequence begins again starting at three.
      Step 2 The middle arrow alternates from being shorter than the others to being the same length.
      Step 3 The number of black dots increases by one each time.
      As it is the fifth in the sequence, the missing box must have two black arrows, a short middle arrow and four black dots:

7 d Step 1 The diagonal cross alternates in size.

      Step 2 The horizontal line alternates in length from one box to the next. The vertical line remains the same length.
      Step 3 The shading moves towards the centre one square at a time, then moves back out one square at a time.

      As it is the fifth in the sequence, the missing box must have a shorter diagonal cross, a longer horizontal line, and a shaded outer square:

8 b The stripes in each section of the shape rotate 45° clockwise each time.
9 e The boxes are grouped into pairs.

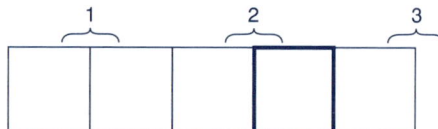

      Step 1 Each pair has one more dollar sign ($) and one more pound sign (£) than the preceding pair.
      Step 2 The first box of each pair is rotated 180° to form the second box of that pair.

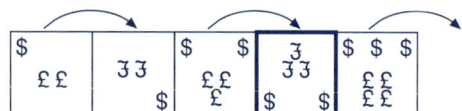

      As it is the fourth in the sequence, the missing box must have two dollar signs in the bottom of the box and three inverted pound signs as shown above.
10 b Step 1 Each box contains a different set of shapes. The three linked shapes are always on a diagonal from top right to bottom left.
      Step 2 The pattern alternates so that the striped shapes become clear and the clear shapes become striped.
      Step 3 The middle shape alternates from being in front of the other two shapes to being behind them.
      As it is the third in the sequence, the missing box must have two striped circles sitting diagonally from top right to bottom left and the middle circle must be behind the other two:

11 b Each box rotates a quarter turn (90°) anticlockwise to form the next box.
12 c The two shapes in one box swap positions in the next box, i.e., the large outer shape becomes the small inner shape and the small inner shape becomes the large outer shape.
      The missing box must therefore contain a large outer square with a smaller inner shape.

Section 4

B 9

Practice 1

    d First letter: represents the inner shape.

       R   S

       Second letter: represents the outer shape.

       X   Y

       The answer is SY because there is no inner shape (S) and the outer shape is a circle (Y).

Practice 2

    a First letter: represents the outer shape.

       P   Q

       Second letter: represents the number of inner lines:
       E = 2
       F = 1
       G = 0
       The answer is QE because the outer shape is a hexagon (Q) and there are two inner lines (E).

1   b First letter: represents the position of the arrows.

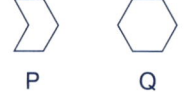
       L   M   N

       Second letter: represents whether the arrows are bold (F) or not (G).
       The answer is NF because the arrows are directly opposite each other (N) and are bold (F).

2   b First letter: represents the angle of the bar.

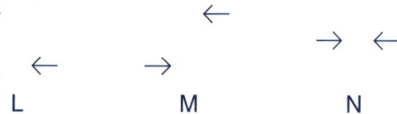
       S   T   U

       Second letter: represents the number of shaded sections:
       C = 2 sections
       D = 3 sections
       E = 1 section
       The answer is TC because the bar is tilted to the right (T) and has two shaded sections (C).

3   c First letter: represents the shaded inner shape.

       D   E   F

       Second letter: represents the number of squares.

       X   Y   Z

       The answer is EY because the shaded inner shape is a circle (E) and there is only one square (Y).

4   e First letter: represents whether the arrow is pointing up (A) or down (B).

Second letter: represents the shading of the circles:
G = inner circle clear, outer circles shaded
H = inner circle shaded, outer circles clear
The answer is BH because the arrow is pointing down (B) and the inner circle is shaded but the outer circles are clear (H).

5 e First letter: represents whether the two shapes at the ends of the line are the same (S) or different (T).
Second letter: represents whether the shapes have a pattern inside them and are joined by a vertical line (K) or whether they are empty and joined by a horizontal line (J).
The answer is SK because the two shapes are the same (S), they have a pattern inside them and are joined by a vertical line (K).

6 a First letter: represents the outer shape.

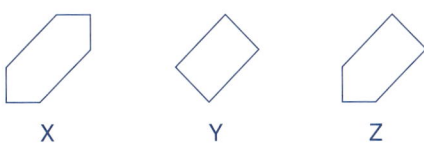

X   Y   Z

Second shape: represents whether the inner symbol is ? (L) or ! (M).
The answer is XM because the outer shape is a hexagon (X) and the inner symbol is an exclamation mark (M).

7 d First letter: represents whether the shape:
• is empty and sits vertically (J)
• contains a line and sits horizontally (K)
• contains a line and sits vertically (L).
Second letter: represents whether the shape is small (R) or large (S).
The answer is KS because the shape contains a line and sits horizontally (K) and is large in size (S).

8 b First letter: represents the direction of the arrow.

D   E   F   G

Second letter: represents whether the inner bar is shaded (R) or unshaded (S).
The answer is ER because the arrow is pointing to the left (E) and the inner bar is shaded (R).

9 b First letter: represents the shape of the lines.

H   I   J

Second letter: represents the size of each shape in a pair:
V = different sizes
W = same size
The answer is IV because each shape is a reversed S (I) and the two shapes are different sizes (V).

10 c First letter: represents the position of the square:
C = top left
D = bottom right
E = centre
Second letter: represents whether the diagonal line is thin (F) or thick (G).
The answer is DG because the square is located in the bottom right (D) and the line is thick (G).

11 c First letter: represents the outer shape.

J   K

Second letter: represents the inner symbol.

R   S   T

The answer is KR because the outer shape is a rectangle (K) and the inner symbol is an arrow (R).

12 c First letter: represents whether the shading is striped (I), light grey (J) or black (K).
Second letter: represents which segment is shaded.

T   U   V   W

The answer is JW because the shading is light grey (J) and the lower left segment is shaded (W).

Section 5

Practice 1
d The bottom row is a horizontal reflection (flipped over version) of the top row.

Practice 2
e Each row has one of each of the three shapes.

1 e Step 1 Each box in a row has the same central shape:
Top Row = circle
Middle Row = triangle
Bottom Row = square
Step 2 The top half of each shape is unshaded and the bottom half is shaded.
Step 3 The lines are the same for each box in a column:
Left column = 1 vertical line (|)
Middle column = 1 diagonal line from top right to bottom left (/)
Right column = 2 diagonal lines from top right to bottom left (//) and 1 diagonal line from top left to bottom right (\)
The missing box must contain a square with the top half unshaded, with two diagonal lines from top right to bottom left and one line from top left to bottom right:

2 b The shape from the first box in a row is rotated 90° clockwise.
3 a Step 1 The largest shape in the first box in each row is rotated 180° and then shaded.

Step 2 The smaller version of the same shape increases in size and is rotated 180°.

Step 3 The thickness of the lines does not change from the box on the left to the box on the right.
Step 4 The smallest shape increases in size slightly and links the other two shapes.
The missing box must therefore look like this:

4 d The shapes in the top row are reflected horizontally (flipped over) and the solid lines that form the letters become dashed.

5 c   Step 1 The objects in the box in the first column are moved to the dotted line in the box in the second column.

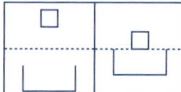

Step 2 Each object is copied, reflected horizontally (flipped over) and placed on the opposite side of the dotted line.

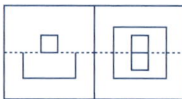

6 d The boxes in the middle row contain the objects from both the top and bottom rows. The position of each object remains the same.

7 b   Step 1 The boxes in the same row contain the same shapes.
Step 2 The shading of the smallest central shape in the right-hand column becomes clear in the left-hand column.

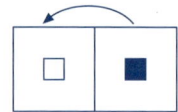

Step 3 The striped background in the right-hand column becomes clear in the left-hand column.

Step 4 The clear outer shape in the right-hand column becomes striped in the left-hand column.

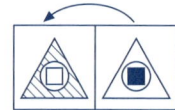

8 a   Step 1 Each row consists of a solid shape, a group of x's and a star-like shape.
Step 2 The shape made of solid lines can be formed by connecting the outline of the shapes in the other two boxes.

The missing box must contain a group of x's that, when joined together, correctly form the hexagon as shown above.

9 a   Step 1 The diagonal shape in the right-hand box is repeated in the left-hand box but with the bottom arrow removed.

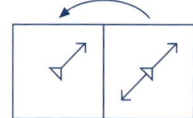

Step 2 The shape in the top left corner in the right-hand box becomes unshaded and crossed through in the left-hand box.

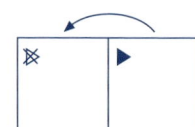

Step 3 The shape in the bottom right corner in the right-hand box moves to the bottom left corner and becomes shaded in the left-hand box.

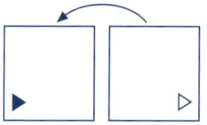

The missing box must therefore look like this:

10 d   Step 1 Each row has a different shape. The number of shapes increases by one in each column.
Step 2 There is one shape in the left-hand column, which is shaded black.
Step 3 The two shapes in the middle column overlap. The area where they overlap is unshaded (highlighted by dashed lines on the diagram below).

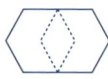

Step 4 The three shapes in the right-hand column also overlap. The top half of the third shape overlaps the middle of the other two shapes. Only the area where all three shapes overlap remains unshaded (highlighted by dashed lines on the diagram below).

The missing box must therefore look like this:

11 d Each box rotates 90° anticlockwise.

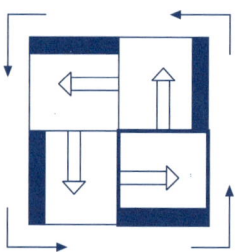

12 c   Step 1 Each row has a different shape. The size of the shape increases with each column.
Step 2 The number of lines increases by one with each column.
Step 3 The lines in the third box in a row are made up of the lines in the first two boxes.

The missing box must therefore look like this:

Test 2
Section 1

Practice 1
    e   The shaded inner shape becomes unshaded and the unshaded inner shape becomes shaded.

Practice 2
    b   The right-hand side of the shape becomes indented.

1   e   Step 1 The shapes are rotated 90° clockwise.

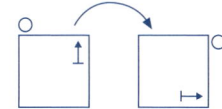

          Step 2 The shapes are reflected vertically (flipped to the left).

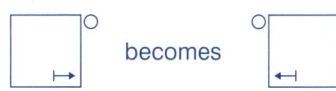

2   c   Step 1 Solid lines remain solid and dashed lines remain dashed.
          Step 2 The inside shape is moved from the centre to one of the corners and duplicated in the other corners.

3   e   Step 1 The shape is rotated 150° clockwise.

          Step 2 The shaded inner shape becomes unshaded. The other shape remains the same.

4   e   The shapes remain the same except that the dashed lines become solid and the solid lines become dashed.

5   c   Step 1 The overall shape is enlarged slightly.
          Step 2 The border of the shape is made up of smaller versions of the overall shape, which for the missing pattern is a square.

6   d   Step 1 The arrow is rotated 90° anticlockwise.

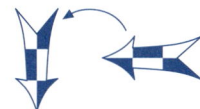

          Step 2 The arrow is reduced in size.
          Step 3 The shading on the different sections of the arrow is swapped so that the unshaded sections become shaded and the shaded sections become unshaded.

7   b   Step 1 The large shape is reflected in a vertical mirror line and the two shapes are joined.

          Step 2 The small shape is placed in the centre of the large shape and becomes striped.

8   d   Step 1 The shape is copied and reflected vertically (flipped to the right).

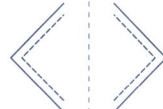

          Step 2 The dashed inner line becomes solid and the solid outer line becomes dashed.

9   c   The shape remains the same but is reduced in size.

10 a   Step 1 The overall shape is rotated 90°.

          Step 2 The individual sections of the overall shape are joined together.

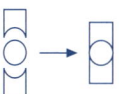

          Step 3 The central section becomes striped.
          Step 4 The shape is placed in a frame that is the same shape as the central section. In the missing shape this would be a circle.
          The missing shape must therefore look like this:

11 b   Step 1 The central shape stays in the same position.
          Step 2 The small shapes at the vertices rotate.

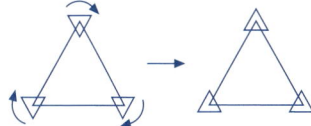

          Step 3 The lines of the smaller and the larger shapes are visible where the shapes overlap as shown above.

12 a   Step 1 The overall shape is rotated 90° clockwise:

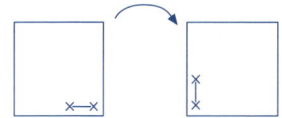

          Step 2 The solid outer line becomes dashed.

Section 2

Practice 1
    b   The pattern is a hammer shape with no base and a rectangular head.

Practice 2
    d   The inner shape is a square. The outer shape has one right angle (90°) and is a mixture of straight and curved lines.

1   e   Step 1 The outer shape is an oval.
          Step 2 The inner shapes are a circle and square which are linked and a pentagon (five sides) which sits separately.

2   b   The large shape is a triangle. Each triangle has a small, a medium and a large version of the same shape. The medium-sized shape is unshaded and the small and large shapes are shaded.

3   a   The individual shapes that make up the overall shape are identical.

4   e   The outer shape is a hexagon made up of dashed lines. It contains a tick mark, an 'x' and a question mark.

5   a   The outer line of the square is solid and the inner line is dashed. The inner shapes consist of two shaded squares and one unshaded square.

6   d   Step 1 Each large shape is divided in half by a dashed line.
          Step 2 Small circles are placed behind each vertex of the large shape.
          Step 3 In the areas where the circles and the large shape overlap, the line of the circle is hidden.

7 c The shapes have a vertical line of symmetry (both sides of a line drawn down the middle of the shape are the same).

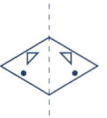

8 b Step 1 One of the three inner shapes is a smaller copy of the outer shape.
Step 2 The other inner shapes are a shaded triangle and an unshaded circle.

9 e Each overall shape has a small, a medium and a large rectangle. One of the rectangles is intersected by the other two rectangles. These two rectangles do not intersect each other.

10 c Step 1 Each overall shape is made up of two versions of the same shape.
Step 2 Each version contains a small square that has one half shaded and one half unshaded.
Step 3 The two versions are the same; however one has been rotated 180°.

11 b Each ring has a small, a medium and a large version of the same shape. The medium-sized shape is unshaded and the largest and smallest shapes are shaded.

12 b The shapes have a vertical line of symmetry (both sides of a line drawn down the middle of the shape are the same).

Section 3

Practice 1
e The sequence is two pictures that alternate.

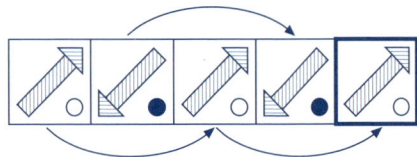

The direction of the stripes remains the same.

Practice 2
a The number of stars and the number of solid straight edges increase by one each time.

1 a The striped shading moves from one square to the next in a clockwise direction each time. The direction of the stripes remains the same.

2 c Step 1 The diagonal square loses a side in an anticlockwise direction each time.

Step 2 The central square is divided into four boxes, one of which is shaded. This shading moves in an anticlockwise direction from one box to the next.

As it is the third in the sequence, the missing box must therefore look like this:

3 d A new larger square is added each time.

4 b The sequence is made up of four shapes: a square, a cross, a triangle and a circle. The number of each of the shapes in a box ranges from 0 to 3.
Step 1 The number of each of the shapes is repeated in two consecutive boxes; however, sometimes the first or second of these boxes isn't shown in the sequence. Instead, if more of the sequence were shown, the box would be placed at either end. For example:

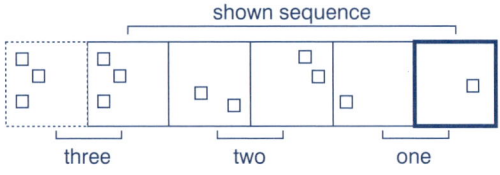

Step 2 The number of each of the shapes then increases or decreases by one from one pair of boxes to the next. Again, sometimes the first or second of these boxes doesn't appear in the given sequence but, if more of the sequence were shown, it would be placed at either end.
The location of the shapes in a box does not matter. The sequence for each of the shapes is therefore:
Square

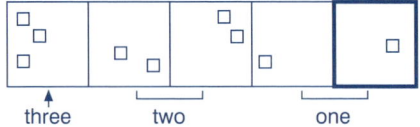

Cross

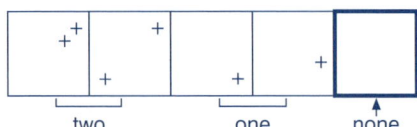

Triangle

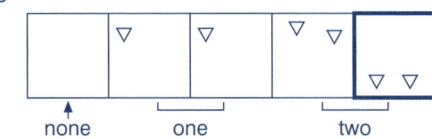

Circle

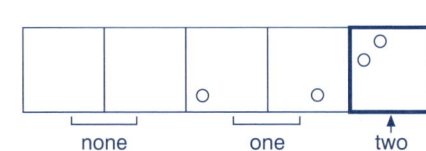

As it is the fifth in the sequence, the missing box must therefore look like this:

5 d Step 1 The large triangle in each box is repeated every third box.

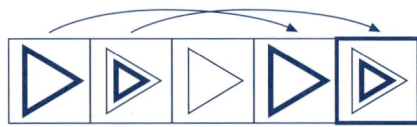

Step 2 The small outer triangle is inverted (flipped over) from one box to the next.
Step 3 The small outer triangle remains on the same side of the large triangle for the first pair of boxes, then moves to the next side in a clockwise direction for each of the following pairs.

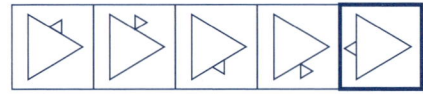

As it is the fifth in the sequence, the missing box must therefore look like this:

6 a The shape alternates between being large and small and is rotated 90° anticlockwise each time.

7 d The overall shape is rotated 90° clockwise each time. As the missing box is the first in the sequence, it must have been used to form box 2. Box 1 is, therefore, formed by rotating box 2 90° *anticlockwise*.

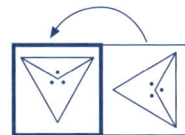

Box 1   Box 2

8 e Step 1 The shapes rotate 45° anticlockwise each time.

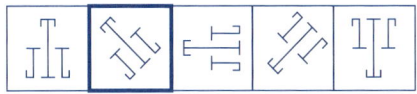

Step 2 Additionally, the J-shapes are inverted (flipped over) each time.

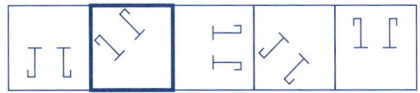

As it is the second in the sequence, the missing box must therefore look like this:

9 c Step 1 The black pencil shape rotates 45° clockwise each time.

Step 2 The small rectangle alternates between being striped and clear.
Step 3 The small rectangle moves clockwise around the pencil, landing on the next side each time.

10 d Step 1 The number of short, diagonal lines decreases by one each time.
Step 2 The number of triangles increases by one each time. The first time a new triangle is added it is unshaded. Each time after that, a triangle is added to the centre of the row and is shaded. As such, the shaded triangles are bordered on each end by a white triangle.

Step 3 The number of squares increases by one each time. The first time a square is added it is unshaded. Each square after that is shaded and added between the two unshaded squares.

As it is the fourth in the sequence, the missing box must therefore look like this:

11 a Step 1 The arrow shape rotates 45° anticlockwise each time.

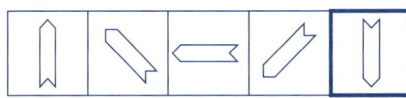

Step 2 The other shape also rotates 45° anticlockwise. The direction of the ends alternates between pointing outwards and pointing inwards.

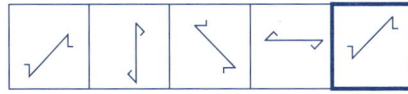

As it is the fifth in the sequence, the missing box must therefore look like this:

12 a The lines of the cross extend one square at a time until they reach the outer square, then reduce in length one square at a time.
The missing square must therefore look like this:

Section 4

Practice 1

d First letter: represents the inner shape.

◆   (nothing)
R   S

Second letter: represents the outer shape.

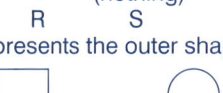

X   Y

The answer is SY because there is no inner shape (S) and the outer shape is a circle (Y).

Practice 2

a First letter: represents the outer shape.

P   Q

Second letter: represents the number of inner lines:
E = 2
F = 1
G = 0
The answer is QE because the outer shape is a hexagon (Q) and there are two inner lines (E).

1 c First letter: represents the location of the line:
P = top
Q = middle
R = bottom
Second letter: represents whether the line is horizontal (U) or vertical (V).
The answer is QU because the line is in the middle (Q) and is horizontal (U).

2 b First letter: represents the direction of the outer shape.

M   N   O

Second letter: represents whether the inner rectangle is striped (D) or shaded black (E).
The answer is NE because the outer shape points right (N) and the inner rectangle is shaded black (E).

3 e First letter: represents whether the small shape is a square (T) or a circle (U).
      Second letter: represents whether the symbol is made up of one version of a shape (H) or two (I).
      Third letter: represents whether the small shape is unshaded (E) or shaded (F).
      The answer is UIF because the small shape is a circle (U), the symbol is made up of two circles (I) and the small circle is shaded (F).

4 e First letter: represents the position of the shapes:
      F = top row
      G = bottom row
      H = middle row
      Second letter: represents which of the three shapes is striped:
      S = shape on the right
      T = shape on the left
      U = shape in the middle
      The answer is HT because the shapes are located in the middle (H) and the shape on the left is striped (T).

5 e First letter: represents whether the shape is unshaded (S) or striped (T).
      Second letter: represents the position of the arrow:
      M = far left
      N = centre
      O = far right
      The answer is TM because the shape is striped (T) and the arrow is positioned on the far left (M).

6 a First letter: represents whether the cross is medium-sized (T), large (U) or small (V).
      Second letter: represents whether the square is large (G), small (H) or medium-sized (I).
      The answer is TI because the cross is medium-sized (T) and the square is also medium-sized (I).

7 d First letter: represents whether the sections of the shapes that don't overlap are striped (G) or unshaded (H).
      Second letter: represents whether the section where the two shapes overlap is unshaded (P), striped (Q) or black (R).
      The answer is HP because the section where the two shapes don't overlap is unshaded (H) and the section where they do overlap is unshaded (P).

8 d First letter: represents the direction of the arrows.

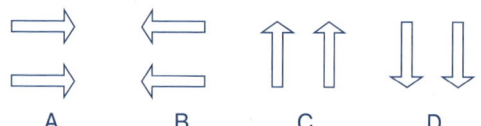

A   B   C   D

      Second letter: represents whether both arrows are shaded (N), both arrows are unshaded (O), or one arrow is shaded (P).
      The answer is CP because the arrows point upwards (C) and one of the arrows is shaded (P).

9 c First letter: represents whether there is an inner circle (E) or not (D).
      Second letter: represents the position of the arrow and the direction in which it is pointing.

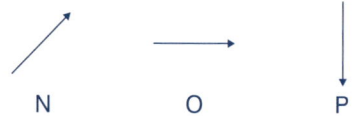

N   O   P

      The answer is DO because there is no inner circle (D) and the horizontal arrow is pointing to the right (O).

10 b First letter: represents whether the inner shape is a rectangle (Q), a cross (R) or a square (S).
      Second letter: represents the position of the trapezium (outer shape).

E   F   G   H

      The answer is QH because the inner shape is a rectangle (Q) and the trapezium's shortest side is on the right (H).

11 c First letter: represents the location of the black square:
      L = bottom
      M = middle
      N = top
      Second letter: represents whether the size of the semi-circle is large (A), small (B) or medium (C).
      The answer is MC because the black square is located in the middle (M) and the semi-circle is medium-sized (C).

12 d First letter: represents whether the size of the triangle is small (N), large (O) or medium (P).
      Second letter: represents whether the inner line is horizontal (S), vertical (T) or diagonal (U).
      The answer is OU because the triangle is large (O) and the horizontal line is diagonal (U).

Section 5

Practice 1
   d The bottom row is a horizontal reflection (flipped over version) of the top row.

Practice 2
   e Each row has one of each of the three shapes.

1 c Step 1 The central symbol from the first box in each row is repeated and gets larger in the second box.

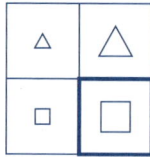

      Step 2 The two symbols inside the bottom shape in the left-hand column are removed and placed to the left of the central symbol in the right-hand column. The frame for these two symbols is discarded.

      Step 3 The top rounded bar is made smaller and the diagonal lines of the two inner symbols are deleted. These two symbols are then placed to the right of the central symbol.

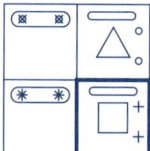

      The missing box must therefore look like this:

2 b Each box in the first column must contain a circle, a square and a hexagon. Working from right to left, each shape alternates from being shaded to unshaded.
      Step 1 The shape in the right-hand column is repeated in the middle column and a second shape is added and shaded black.
      Step 2 The shapes in the middle column are repeated in the left-hand column and a third outer shape is added and shaded black.
      Step 3 The boxes in each column contain the same number of lines:
              First column = 4 lines
              Second column = 3 lines
              Third column = 2 lines
              The length and direction of the lines is the same within each column. The lines are always placed underneath the central shapes.

As the middle column contains a hexagon and a circle, the third outer shape to be added to the missing box must be a shaded square.
The missing box must therefore look like this:

3 a The symbols in the top row are reflected horizontally (flipped over) in the bottom row. The lower inner shape is then shaded.
4 a Working from left to right, the symbols in each box are rotated 180°. Therefore, the symbols in the left-hand and right-hand boxes of each row are the same.
5 a The pattern of the top row is repeated in the third row.
6 a Step 1 The large shape in the bottom row is reflected horizontally (flipped over along the dashed line shown below) and the shaded section becomes unshaded.

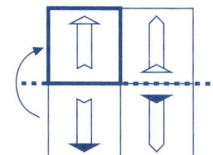

Step 2 The two smaller shapes in the right-hand column are reflected vertically (flipped over along the dashed line shown below).

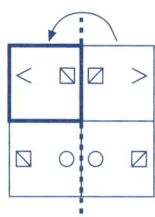

The missing box must therefore look like this:

7 e Step 1 The stars in each column have the same shading:
Left column: black
Middle column: striped
Right column: grey
Step 2 As they proceed down the columns, each star is rotated 90° clockwise. The same point remains shaded.

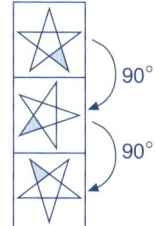

8 c Each row has three versions of the same shape.
Step 1 The size of the shape in each row increases from one box to the next.
Step 2 Each row has one shape that is unshaded, one that is shaded black and one that is striped.
The missing box must therefore contain a medium-sized striped triangle.
9 b Step 1 The boxes in the right-hand column are rotated 180° and repeated in the left-hand column.
Step 2 The solid lines become dashed and the dashed lines become solid.
The missing box must therefore look like this:

10 d Step 1 Each column has a square, a triangle and a hexagon.
Step 2 The top row contains small shapes, the middle row contains medium-sized shapes and the bottom row contains large shapes.
The missing box must therefore contain a medium-sized hexagon.
11 a The bottom image is a horizontal reflection of the top image.
12 b The shapes in the top row rotate 45° clockwise as they move down the column.

Test 3
Section 1

Practice 1
e The shaded inner shape becomes unshaded and the unshaded inner shape becomes shaded.
Practice 2
b The right-hand side of the shape becomes indented.
1 b The overall shape is rotated 90° clockwise and the shading is removed.
2 d Step 1 The two small shapes are moved inwards so that they rest on the lines of the larger shape.
Step 2 The small shape on the right is rotated 180° and its lines become dashed instead of solid. This shape then becomes transparent.
3 d The outer lines beyond the diagonal lines shown below are removed, leaving only the three inner lines of each shape.

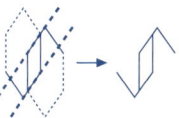

4 c Step 1 The three overall shapes are reflected horizontally (flipped over) and then joined together.
Step 2 The shading of the three identical shapes is reversed.
5 e Step 1 The overall shape (including the letter at the bottom) is copied and reflected vertically (flipped to the right).

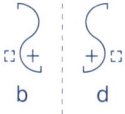

Step 2 The small shapes swap places.

Step 3 The type of line used for the small shapes is swapped so that the dashed line becomes solid and the solid line becomes dashed.

6 c Step 1 The overall shape is rotated 180°.

Step 2 The lines change from solid to dashed.
Step 3 A solid line border is added around the dashed shape.
Step 4 A small circle is placed below the bottom line of the border.

7 c Step 1 The first shape of the first pair is rotated 90° clockwise to form the first shape of the second pair.

Step 2 The second shape of the first pair is rotated 180° to form the second shape of the second pair.

8 c The overall shape is rotated 90° anticlockwise and the largest of the individual shapes is shaded.
9 a The pieces fit together as if parts of a jigsaw puzzle.
10 a Step 1 The diagonal stripes are removed from the smaller shape.
Step 2 A larger dashed outline of the same shape is placed around the smaller shape.
11 d Step 1 The shape is rotated 90° clockwise.

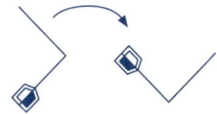

Step 2 An arrowhead is added to the end of the line that is empty.

Step 3 The inner part of the shape at the end of the other line is removed, leaving the outer frame.

Step 4 The part that was removed moves to the bottom of the line with the arrowhead and has its shading reversed.

12 a Step 1 The outer frame of the grid becomes thicker.
Step 2 The left-hand column remains the same.
Step 3 The shapes at the top of the middle and right-hand columns move to the bottom row.

Section 2

Practice 1
d The others all have the shortest side of the trapezium (the large shape) at the top.
Practice 2
c The other shapes have sides that are all the same length.
1 c The other arrows all travel in a clockwise direction around the inside of the square.
2 c The others all have the two unshaded squares close to each other but in option c the two unshaded squares are separated by the shaded square.
3 c The others all have different shapes at the ends of each line, whereas this option has the same shape at both ends.
4 c The others all have one black square in the smallest section of the divided rectangle.
5 a All of the other shapes are symmetrical.
6 a It is the only one with the same number of horizontal lines as stars (two of each).
7 e The others all have the same number of short horizontal lines as there are vertical lines, whereas option e has four short horizontal lines but only three vertical lines.
8 e The others all have a bold line in between two thinner lines, whereas this option has one thin line in between two bold lines.

9 b The others have more ticks than crosses, whereas in this option there are more crosses than ticks.
10 e The two smaller shapes overlap the larger shape for all symbols except in option e, where the small unshaded shape is placed next to the larger shape.
11 a The others all have three lines meeting inside the shape, whereas this option has four lines.
12 b In the others, the dashed line separates shaded and unshaded squares, whereas this option has two shaded squares and one unshaded square on the same side of the dashed line.

Section 3

Practice 1
e The sequence is two pictures that alternate.

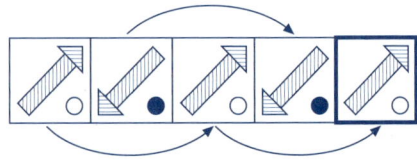

Practice 2
a The number of stars and the number of solid straight edges increase by one each time.
1 d Step 1 The unshaded area inside the rectangle moves from left to right in three steps, then the pattern starts again.

Step 2 The number of shaded rhombuses (diamond shapes) below the rectangle decreases from 3 to 0 in three steps, then the pattern starts again.

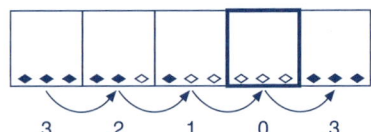

The missing box must therefore look like this:

2 d Step 1 The direction of the large outer arrow alternates from pointing upwards to pointing downwards from one box to the next. Its style also alternates from having a solid line to a dashed line.
Step 2 The direction of the small inner shape alternates from pointing downwards to pointing upwards from one pair of boxes to the next pair. Its style also alternates from having a dashed line to a solid line from one box to the next.
The missing box must therefore look like this:

3 e Step 1 The diagonal lines are reflected vertically (flipped to the right) from one box to the next.
Step 2 The inner rectangle alternates from lying vertically to lying horizontally in the centre of the box.
Step 3 The shading of the rectangle is split into three equal sections. The shading decreases by one section at a time until only one shaded section is left. The shading then starts to increase by one section at a time.

The missing box must therefore look like this:

4 c Step 1 The shape alternates from being a hexagon to a rhombus (diamond shape).
         Step 2 Each shape has one central horizontal line and the number of vertical lines inside each shape increases by one each time.
         The missing box must contain a hexagon, with one central horizontal line and four vertical lines:

5 c Step 1 The number of horizontal lines and shaded circles increases by one each time.
         Step 2 The position of the shaded circles alternates from being placed on the right-hand end of each line to the left-hand end.
         The missing box must therefore look like this:

6 b Step 1 The square remains in the same position in each box.
         Step 2 The circle moves in a clockwise direction from one box to the next. The area where the two shapes overlap is shaded.
         The missing box must therefore look like this:

7 a Step 1 The number of shaded squares decreases by one each time from alternate sides.
         Step 2 The number of horizontal lines increases by one each time, alternating from being added below to above the ellipse (oval shape).
         The missing box must have the middle three squares in the ellipse shaded, and two horizontal lines – one above the ellipse and one below:

8 d Step 1 Each group of shapes moves around the box, from one corner to the next, in a clockwise direction.
         Step 2 One circle is removed from the group of circles, becomes shaded, and replaces a square in the group of squares each time.
         Step 3 The replaced square is shaded and moves ahead to the next corner.
         The missing box must therefore look like this:

9 c Step 1 The square containing the cross moves clockwise half a side each time.
         Step 2 The square containing the circle moves clockwise from one corner to the next.
         The missing box must therefore look like this:

10 a Step 1 The number of small arrows decreases by one each time. The small arrows always point downwards.
         Step 2 The number of horizontal lines on the large arrow decreases by one each time. The direction of the arrow alternates from pointing upwards to pointing downwards.

The missing box must show one large arrow pointing upwards with two horizontal lines, next to two small arrows pointing downwards:

11 d Step 1 The overall shape rotates 90° anticlockwise each time.
         Step 2 The shaded section of the rhombus (diamond shape) alternates between the two triangles that are touching the unshaded rectangle.
         The missing box must therefore look like this:

12 b The sequence is made up of two alternating boxes. The missing box will therefore look the same as the second box.

Section 4

Practice 1
   d First letter: represents the inner shape.

R   S

Second letter: represents the outer shape.

X   Y

The answer is SY because there is no inner shape (S) and the outer shape is a circle (Y).

Practice 2
   a First letter: represents the outer shape.

P   Q

Second letter: represents the number of inner lines:
E = 2
F = 1
G = 0
The answer is QE because the outer shape is a hexagon (Q) and there are two inner lines (E).

1 b First letter: represents whether the shape is a square (J) or a triangle (K).
      Second letter: represents the position of the shape that is shaded:
      V = middle
      W = top
      X = bottom
      The answer is JX because the shape is made up of squares (J) and the bottom square is shaded (X).

2 a First letter: represents the inner symbol:
      F = ◥
      G = ▯ ▯
      H = ✕
      Second letter: represents whether the hexagon is small (A) or large (B).
      The answer is FB because the inner shape is ◥ (F) and the outer shape is a large hexagon (B).

3 c First letter: represents the type of shape used to make the pattern.

R   S   T

Second letter: represents whether the pattern is pointing to the left (V) or to the right (W).
Third letter: represents whether there are two shapes (E) or three shapes (F).

The answer is TWE because the pattern: is made up of rhombuses (diamond shapes) (T); is pointing to the right (W); and is made up of two shapes (E).

4 c First letter: represents the shape used to make the pattern:
E = ■
F = ○
G = L
Second letter: represents whether there are three shapes (A), one shape (B) or two shapes (C).
Third letter: represents whether the shapes are shaded (J) or unshaded (H).
The answer is FBJ because the shape is a circle (F), there is only one (B) and it is shaded (J).

5 d First letter: represents the position of the crosses on the line:
R = top
S = bottom
T = middle
Second letter: represents whether there are three crosses (C), one cross (D), or two crosses (E).
The answer is TD because the cross is in the middle of the line (T) and there is only one cross (D).

6 b First letter: represents the position of the hexagon.

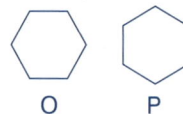

O   P

Second letter: represents whether there are two lines (H) or three lines (I) inside the hexagon.
Third letter: represents whether one inner section of the hexagon is shaded (T) or all sections are unshaded (U).
The answer is OIT because the top and bottom of the hexagon are flat (O), it has three inner lines (I) and one inner section is shaded (T).

7 e First letter: represents whether the shape is a square (J), rectangle (K) or triangle (L).
Second letter: represents whether the inner stripes are diagonal (R) or horizontal (S).
Third letter: represents whether the inner stripes are solid (B) or broken (C).
The answer is KSC because it is a rectangle (K) with horizontal inner stripes (S) which are broken (C).

8 a First letter: represents the inner shape.

I   J   K

Second letter: represents the position of the inner shape:
V = bottom left
W = top right
X = bottom right
The answer is IW because the hexagon (I) is in the top right corner of the square (W).

9 c First letter: represents whether the hexagon is striped (H) or unshaded (I).
Second letter: represents whether the hexagon is at the top (R), the bottom (S) or the middle (T).
The answer is HT because the hexagon is striped (H) and placed in the middle row (T).

10 e First letter: represents the thickness of the outer line of the circle.

D   E   F

Second letter: represents the direction of the stripes:
X = diagonal
Y = vertical
Z = horizontal
The answer is FX because the circle has a thick outer line (F) and diagonal stripes (X).

11 a First letter: represents the direction in which the outer shape is pointing.

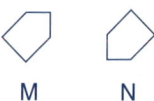

M   N

Second letter: represents the number of shaded squares inside the shape:
X = 1
Y = 2
Z = 0
The answer is NX because the shape is pointing downwards (N) and has one shaded square inside (X).

12 d First letter: represents whether the large triangle contains a black shaded section (G) or not (F).
Second letter: represents the direction the large triangle is pointing:
A = upwards
B = to the left
C = downwards
The answer is GC because the large triangle has one black section (G) and is pointing downwards (C).

Section 5

Practice 1
d   The bottom row is a horizontal reflection (flipped over version) of the top row.

Practice 2
e   Each row has one of each of the three shapes.

1 a Step 1 The pattern in the left-hand column is rotated 90° anticlockwise in the right-hand column.

Step 2 A figure eight shape is added at the open end of the shape.
The missing box must look like this:

2 c The pattern in the top box is repeated in the bottom box.

3 e The top row contains rhombuses (diamond shapes), the middle row contains hexagons and the bottom row contains circles.
Step 1 Each row has a large, medium and small version of its shape.
Step 2 Each shape is divided in half by a straight line: the rhombuses by a vertical line; the hexagons by a diagonal line and the circles by a horizontal line.
Step 3 The position of the inner shape in each row, alternates from one side of the dividing line to the other.
Step 4 In each row, one of the inner shapes is unshaded, one is striped and one is shaded black.
The missing box must contain a large hexagon, with the inner shape shaded black and placed above the diagonal dividing line:

4 c Step 1 The top section of the shape in the first column increases in size in the second column.

Step 2 The bottom section remains the same size but it becomes shaded black and a horizontal line is drawn through it in the right-hand column.

The missing box must therefore look like this:

5 a Step 1 Each pattern in the top row is repeated in the bottom row.
   Step 2 In the bottom row, the small unshaded triangle flips over from the inside to the outside of the rhombus (diamond shape).

   Step 3 In the bottom row, the small black triangle flips over from the inside to the outside of the rhombus then slides around to the other side of the point.

The missing box must therefore look like this:

6 b Moving from left to right in each row, the number of lines decreases by one each time and the squares alternate between being shaded and unshaded.

7 e Step 1 Each column has three large versions of the same shape and three small versions of the same inner shape:

Column	Large shape	Inner shape
Left	square	triangle
Middle	octagon	square
Right	circle	circle

   Step 2 As you go down each column, a new shape is added to the inner shapes: a hexagon is added in the middle row; a square is added in the bottom row.

The missing box must show a large octagon that contains a small square inside a hexagon, inside a square:

8 a Step 1 Different-sized versions of the same shape are shown in each row:
   Top = triangle
   Middle = square
   Bottom = hexagon
   Step 2 Each shape in the left-hand column is shaded black and has a horizontal line below it. In the middle column, the shapes are striped and have two outer lines that are parallel to the sides of the shape. In the right-hand column, there are two unshaded versions of the same shape, one placed inside the other, and both are made up of solid lines.

The missing box must contain two unshaded hexagons, one placed inside the other, with both being made up of solid lines:

9 c Step 1 Each pattern in the top row is rotated 90° clockwise to form the pattern in the bottom row.
   Step 2 The square is moved slightly to the left.

The missing box must therefore look like this:

10 a The boxes in each column contain different versions of the same shape:
   Left = rhombus (diamond shape)
   Middle = square
   Right = triangle
   Step 1 Each column has one box containing one shape and two boxes containing two of the shapes.
   Step 2 The boxes with two versions have one shaded shape and one unshaded shape. In one box the shaded shape is on the left, and in the other the shaded shape is on the right.
   Step 3 In each column, the shape or shapes are at the top in one box, in the middle in another and at the bottom in another.

The missing box must have two triangles, with the shaded version on the right-hand side, and both shapes placed at the bottom of the box:

11 d The symbol in each box is made up of three connected shapes: a small rectangle, a straight line and a small black circle.
   Step 1 In each row, the straight line is positioned: once diagonally pointing to the top right-hand corner; once diagonally pointing to the top left-hand corner and once vertically.
   Step 2 In each row, the black circle is placed twice at one end of the line and once in the middle of the line.
   Step 3 In each row, the rectangle is placed twice at one end of the line and once in the middle of the line. In the top and bottom rows, the rectangle is unshaded.

The symbol in the missing box must therefore look like this:

12 b The pattern in this matrix works from left to right.
   Step 1 The two shapes on the top row in the left-hand column are copied and reflected horizontally (flipped over). The copies are then attached to the top of the original shapes in the right-hand column.

   Step 2 The left-hand and right-hand shapes in the middle row swap positions, but do not change direction.

The central symbol in the middle row remains unchanged.
   Step 3 The line in the third row is copied and the copy is added below the last line of the pattern.

The missing box must therefore look like this:

Test 4
Section 1

Practice 1
    e   The shaded inner shape becomes unshaded and the unshaded inner shape becomes shaded.

Practice 2
    b   The right-hand side of the shape becomes indented.

1 e Step 1 The first shape is copied and turned horizontally.
       Step 2 The copied shape is placed on top of the original shape. The lines where the shapes overlap show through.

2 b The outer shape is reduced in size and rotated 180°. The inside shape is removed.

3 a The two shapes swap positions.

4 e Step 1 The shape is copied and reflected vertically (flipped to the right).

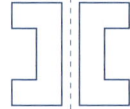

       Step 2 The sections that jut out horizontally become striped.

5 b Step 1 The shape is rotated 90° anticlockwise.

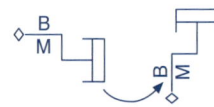

       Step 2 The left-hand letter is rotated so that it is the right way up.

       Step 3 The central line is reflected vertically (flipped to the right).

       Step 4 The small shape at the base of the central line is moved above the first bend.

6 b Step 1 The shape is rotated 180°. The shaded square becomes unshaded.

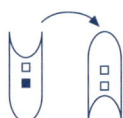

       Step 2 The outline of the original shape is copied, rotated 90° clockwise and placed on top of the original shape.

7 b Step 1 The large shape is reflected vertically (flipped to the right).

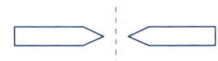

       Step 2 The flag shape is moved to the other end of the large shape.

       Step 3 The lines of the triangular section of the flag shape become dashed.

8 d The overall shape is reflected horizontally (flipped over).

9 b Step 1 The shape is rotated 180° and the shading is removed.

10 a The shape is rotated 180° and reduced in size.

11 e Step 1 The shape is rotated 180°.

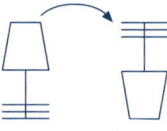

       Step 2 A smaller version of the top section of the original shape is placed inside the larger version.

12 e The overall symbol is made up of 3 shapes:
        A   B   C

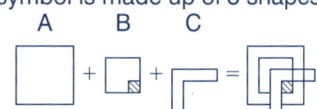

       Step 1 The right-hand section of Shape C is detached at the point where it intersects with Shape B and is moved outside Shape A.

       Step 2 The bottom section of Shape C that overlaps Shape A is removed.

       Step 3 The diagonal shading in Shape B moves from the bottom right-hand corner to fill the rest of Shape B.

Section 2

Practice 1
    d   The others all have the shortest side of the trapezium (the large shape) at the top.

Practice 2
    c   The other shapes have sides that are all the same length.

1 d The others have the same number of slanted lines as small vertical lines, whereas this option has six diagonal lines and eight small vertical lines.

2	d	The other shapes have two diagonal lines of symmetry, whereas this option is not symmetrical because the lower triangle is not centred on the mirror line.
3	d	Each of the other options includes a black square inside a circle.
4	a	When the others are positioned with the straight line at the bottom, the small shaded section is always on the right. In this option, the shading is on the left.
5	e	In the others, the number of 'leaves' on the left of the stem is always greater than the number of 'leaves' on the right-hand side.
6	d	The outer shapes of the other options have five sides whereas the outer shape in this option has six sides.
7	d	The others have five small inner shapes, whereas this option has four.
8	d	

The other options have the shaded circle at the corner of sides A and B, whereas in this option the circle is placed at the corner of sides B and C.

9	d	The other options all contain five circles, whereas this option only has four.
10	e	In the others, the squares are on opposite sides of the circle, whereas in this option the squares are on the same side of the circle.
11	a	The others have a circle in the central rectangle.
12	b	The other options show different rotated versions of the same shape. Option b has been rotated and then reflected.

Section 3

Practice 1

    e   The sequence is two pictures that alternate.

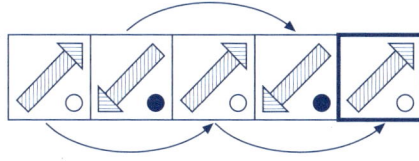

Practice 2

    a   The number of stars and the number of solid straight edges increase by one each time.

1 b Step 1 The letters in the first box are reflected horizontally (flipped over) to form the second box.

Step 2 The letters in the second box are reflected vertically (flipped to the right) to form the third box.

Step 3 The pattern then starts again, so the third box is reflected horizontally to form the fourth box.

2 e Step 1 The number of small horizontal lines increases by one each time. The position of the lines alternates from being in the top left corner of the box to the bottom right corner each time.

Step 2 The diagonal shape is rotated 180° each time from one box to the next.

Step 3 Another U-shaped section is added to the diagonal shape each time.

Step 4 The number of shaded circles at the opposite end of the diagonal shape increases by one each time.

The missing box must therefore look like this:

3 e Step 1 Each box has five shapes. Four of the shapes are shaded black and one is unshaded.

Step 2 The shape that is unshaded moves anticlockwise to the next corner and becomes shaded. The other shape in this corner becomes unshaded. For example:

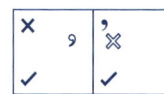

Step 3 This unshaded shape now moves anticlockwise to the next corner and becomes shaded. The other shape in this corner becomes unshaded. For example:

This pattern continues throughout the sequence so the missing box must therefore look like this:

4 a Step 1 The number of triangles in the centre of the box increases by one each time.

Step 2 The small black dot moves forward five squares in a clockwise direction each time.

Step 3 The square in which the small black dot was located is removed in the following box.

The missing box must therefore look like this:

5 c The first three boxes form a repeating block. The missing box will therefore look the same as the first box.

6 c The sequence is made up of two alternating patterns. The missing box therefore relates to boxes 3 and 5. Working from left to right, box 5 is rotated 90° anticlockwise to form box 3. Box 3 is rotated 90° anticlockwise to form box 1.

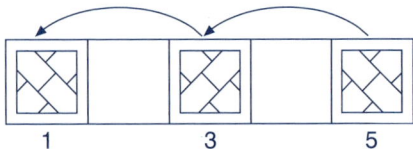

7 e Step 1 One arrow pointing upwards is added each time.
Step 2 One parallelogram is added to the front of the row each time. The new parallelogram always has opposite shading to the parallelogram on its right.

Step 3 One square is added to the bottom right-hand corner of the row of squares each time. The new square always has opposite shading to the square above.

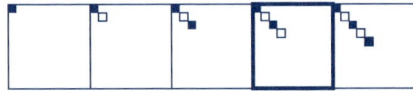

The missing box must therefore look like this:

8 b Step 1 The shapes rotate 90° anticlockwise each time.
Step 2 The number of arrows decreases from three to two to one then back up to three again.

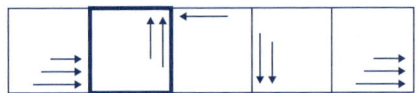

Step 3 The number of small shaded squares decreases from six to five to four then back up to six again.
The missing box must therefore look like this:

9 b Step 1 The boxes are grouped into pairs. The shape in the first box of each pair is reflected horizontally (flipped over) to form the shape in the second box of each pair.

Step 2 In the second box of each pair, the shaded section becomes unshaded and the unshaded secton becomes shaded.
The missing box must therefore look like this:

10 d Step 1 The stripes are removed from one shape each time in the following order:
top left → centre → top right.

Step 2 The black shading moves from one box to the next in the following order:
bottom left → bottom right → top left → centre → top right.

Step 3 Once a shape that was shaded black has become unshaded it is removed.
The missing box must therefore look like this:

11 e The shapes rotate 90° clockwise from one box to the next.

12 c This sequence has two alternating patterns. Each pattern follows the same rule.
Step 1 In the first pattern the contents of box 1 are reflected horizontally (flipped over) to form the contents of box 3. The contents of box 3 are reflected horizontally to form the contents of box 5.

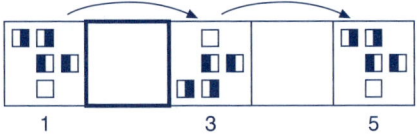

Step 2 In the second pattern, box 4 must have been formed by the contents of box 2 being reflected horizontally (flipped over).

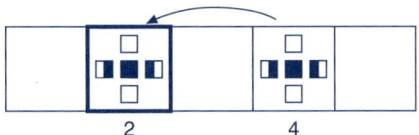

Section 4

Practice 1

d First letter: represents the inner shape.

◆ (nothing)
R   S

Second letter: represents the outer shape.

X   Y

The answer is SY because there is no inner shape (S) and the outer shape is a circle (Y).

Practice 2

a First letter: represents the outer shape.

P   Q

Second letter: represents the number of inner lines:
E = 2
F = 1
G = 0
The answer is QE because the outer shape is a hexagon (Q) and there are two inner lines (E).

1 e First letter: represents whether the arrow is pointing up (A) or down (B).
Second letter: represents whether the two circles attached to the arrowhead are shaded (G) or unshaded (H).
Third letter: represents whether all of the circles are shaded (R) or whether the circles are a mixture of being shaded and unshaded (S).

The answer is BHS because the arrow is pointing down (B), the small circles attached to the arrowhead are unshaded (H) and there is a mixture of shaded and unshaded circles (S).

2 **e** First letter: represents the medium-sized shape.

P Q R S

Second letter: represents whether the @ symbol is the right way up (D) or upside down (E).
Third letter: represents whether there is a large shape (L) or not (M).
The answer is PDM because the medium-sized shape is a hexagon (P), the @ symbol is the right way up (D) and there is no large shape (M).

3 **b** First letter: represents whether there is one internal line (G) or three internal lines (H).
Second letter: represents the direction of the shape.

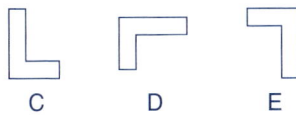
C D E

The answer is GE because there is one internal line (G) and the shape is pointing to the left (E).

4 **d** First letter: represents the number of V shapes.

V W X

Second letter: represents the type of shape that sits inside each V.

F G H

Third letter: represents the number of lines below the V shapes:
A = 2
B = 1
C = 3
The answer is XFB because there is one V shape (X), the shape inside the V is a triangle (F) and there is one line below the V shape (B).

5 **d** First letter: represents the style of the inner shape:
N = unshaded square
O = no inner shape
P = shaded square
Second letter: represents whether the size of the outer square is large (I) or small (J).
The answer is OJ because there is no inner shape (O) and the outer square is small (J).

6 **e** First letter: represents the number and position of the circles:
A = one circle at the top
B = two circles, one at the top and one at the bottom
C = one circle on the intersection of the two lines
Second letter: represents whether the lines of the cross are thin (W) or thick (X).
The answer is CW because there is one circle placed on the intersection of the two lines (C) and the lines of the cross are thin (W).

7 **c** First letter: represents whether the inner letter is c (L), a (M) or e (N).
Second letter: represents whether the overall shape is horizontal (C) or vertical (D).
The answer is LD because the inner letter is a 'c' (L) and the overall shape is vertical (D).

8 **e** First letter: represents the top section of the shape.

L M N

Second letter: represents the bottom section of the shape.

X Y Z

The answer is NZ because the top section of the shape is ⌣ (N) and the bottom section of the shape is ⟋⟍ (Z).

9 **d** First letter: represents the small objects on the points of the larger shape:
M = squares
N = crosses
O = circles
Second letter: represents the larger shape.

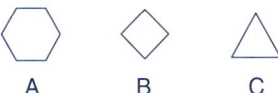
A B C

The answer is OA because the small objects are circles (O) and the overall shape is a hexagon (A).

10 **d** First letter: represents whether the bottom shape is shaded (F) or unshaded (G).
Second letter: represents whether the top shape is striped (P), unshaded (Q) or shaded (R).
The answer is GQ because the bottom section of the shape is unshaded (G) and the top section is unshaded (Q).

11 **a** First letter: represents whether the inner triangle is small (Y) or large (X).
Second letter: represents whether the inner triangle is unshaded (A) or shaded (B).
Third letter: represents whether the outer circle is small (F) or large (G).
The answer is XAG because the inner triangle is large (X) and unshaded (A), and the outer circle is large (G).

12 **b** First letter: represents whether the inner shapes point to the left (M) or the right (N).
Second letter: represents whether the rectangle is vertical (F) or horizontal (G).
Third letter: represents whether the rectangle is striped (R) or unshaded (S).
The answer is MGR because the inner shapes point to the left (M), the rectangle is positioned horizontally (G) and is striped (R).

Section 5

Practice 1
  d The bottom row is a horizontal reflection (flipped over version) of the top row image.

Practice 2
  e Each row has one of each of the three shapes.

1 **e** The symbols in the top row are repeated in the bottom row. The square in the centre of each symbol becomes a circle in the bottom row.

2 **e** Step 1 The shapes in each row rotate 90° clockwise from one box to the next.
Step 2 Each row has one shape with a solid line, one with a broken line and one with a dashed line.
Step 3 Each shape has a shaded inner circle.
The missing box must therefore have a shape that points to the left, which has a solid line and contains a shaded circle:

3 **b** The shapes in the right-hand column are reflections (copies flipped to the right) of the shapes in the left-hand column.
The missing box must therefore look like this:

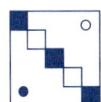

4 **a** Step 1 The shapes in the bottom row are reflections (flipped over versions) of the shapes in the top row.

Step 2 The solid lines of the original shapes become dashed in the reflections. The dashed lines of the original shapes become solid in the reflections.
The missing box must therefore look like this:

5 e Step 1 Each row has two small versions and one large version of the same shape.
Step 2 The shapes in the left- and right-hand columns are divided in half by a straight line that extends beyond the shape.
Step 3 The shapes in the middle column contain three straight lines. These lines follow the same direction as the lines in the other shapes in the row, but they do not extend beyond the shape.
The missing box must therefore look like this:

6 e Step 1 Each row and each column contain a circle, a square and a hexagon.
Step 2 The shapes in each row are the same size:
Top = small
Middle = medium
Bottom = large
The missing box must therefore look like this:

7 d Step 1 The shape in the bottom row is copied and reflected horizontally (flipped over) in the top row.

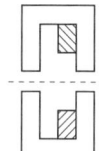

Step 2 Unshaded shapes become shaded and shaded shapes become unshaded.
The missing box must therefore look like this:

8 d The shapes in the left-hand column are copied and reflected vertically (flipped to the right) in the right-hand column.

9 b Step 1 The shapes in the right-hand column are repeated in the left-hand column.
Step 2 The shaded squares become unshaded.
Step 3 The number of triangles and black dots decreases by one.
Step 4 A central line is added between the two angular lines.
The missing box must therefore look like this:

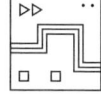

10 d Step 1 The arrow is copied three times, with each copy being placed at 90° intervals. The arrows do not touch each other.

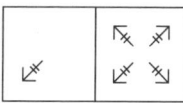

Step 2 The small squares are copied over to the top of the box. The squares are then repeated at the base of the box but, for these copies the shading is reversed.
The missing box must therefore look like this:

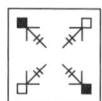

11 c Step 1 The small squares in the boxes in the left-hand column are repeated in the boxes in the right-hand column.
Step 2 Each row has a different style of line.
Top =
Middle =
Bottom =

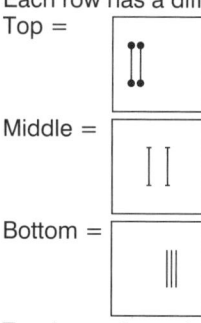

Two boxes in each row have one version of the line or group of lines and one box has two versions.
Step 3 Each row has a different symbol.
Top = ×
Middle = √
Bottom = ?
Step 4 In each box in a row, the symbol is placed in one of three positions: to the left of the lines, to the right of the lines or in between the two versions of the lines. For example:

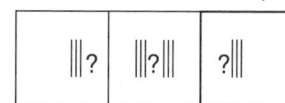

As it is in the right-hand column and is in the bottom row, the missing box must therefore look like this:

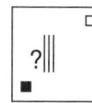

12 a Step 1 The cubes in the top row are reflected horizontally (flipped over) in the bottom row. The circle on the top face of the original cube is removed.

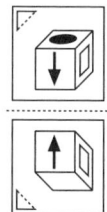

Step 2 The small triangles are also reflected horizontally (flipped over) but the dashed line becomes solid.
The missing box must therefore look like this:

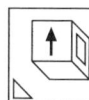

11+
Non-verbal Reasoning

Multiple-choice Test Papers
Pack 1
Test 3

Read the following:

- Do not begin the test or open this booklet until told to do so. Follow the instructions for sitting the test
- Work as quickly and as carefully as you can
- Answers should be marked in the answer booklet provided, not in this test booklet
- You may do rough working on a separate sheet of paper
- Be careful to keep your place in the accompanying answer booklet
- You will have 30 minutes to complete the test

OXFORD
UNIVERSITY PRESS

Great Clarendon Street, Oxford, OX2 6DP, United Kingdom

Oxford University Press is a department of the University of Oxford. It furthers the University's objective of excellence in research, scholarship, and education by publishing worldwide. Oxford is a registered trade mark of Oxford University Press in the UK and in certain other countries

Text © Andrew Baines 2015
Illustrations © Oxford University Press 2015

The moral rights of the authors have been asserted

First published in 2015

All rights reserved. No part of this publication may be reproduced, stored in a retrieval system, or transmitted, in any form or by any means, without the prior permission in writing of Oxford University Press, or as expressly permitted by law, by licence or under terms agreed with the appropriate reprographics rights organization. Enquiries concerning reproduction outside the scope of the above should be sent to the Rights Department, Oxford University Press, at the address above.

You must not circulate this work in any other form and you must impose this same condition on any acquirer

British Library Cataloguing in Publication Data
Data available

978-0-19-274087-8

Paper used in the production of this book is a natural, recyclable product made from wood grown in sustainable forests. The manufacturing process conforms to the environmental regulations of the country of origin.

Printed in China

Acknowledgements

The publishers would like to thank the following for permissions to use copyright material:

Cover illustrations: Lo Cole

Although we have made every effort to trace and contact all copyright holders before publication this has not been possible in all cases. If notified, the publisher will rectify any errors or omissions at the earliest opportunity.

Links to third party websites are provided by Oxford in good faith and for information only. Oxford disclaims any responsibility for the materials contained in any third party website referenced in this work.

The manufacturer's authorised representative in the EU for product safety is Oxford University Press España S.A. of El Parque Empresarial San Fernando de Henares, Avenida de Castilla, 2 – 28830 Madrid (www.oup.es/en or product.safety@oup.com). OUP España S.A. also acts as importer into Spain of products made by the manufacturer.

Section 1

Which shape or pattern on the right completes the second pair in the same way as the first pair?

Example

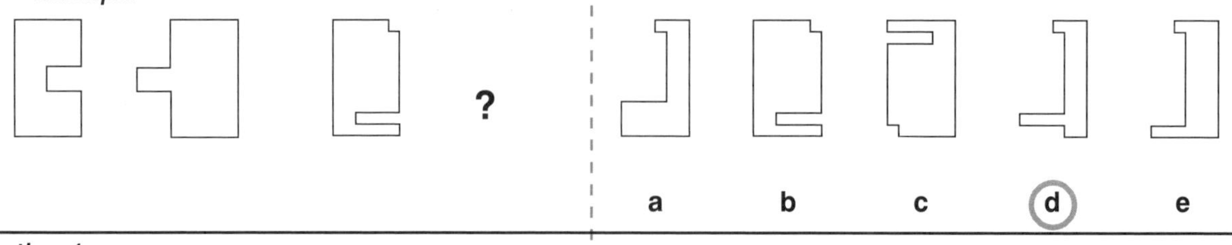

?
a
b
c
d
e

Practice 1

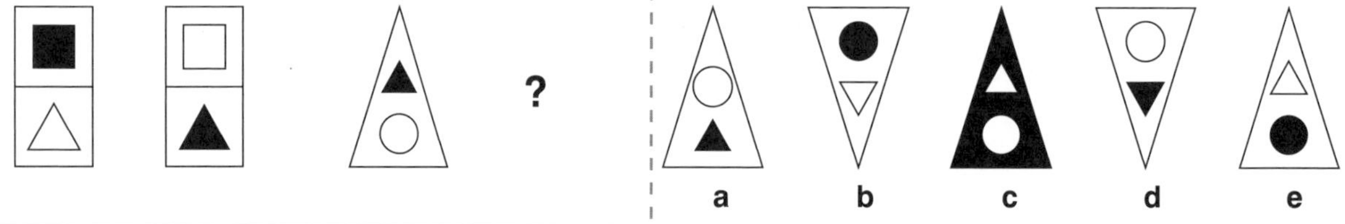

?
a
b
c
d
e

Practice 2

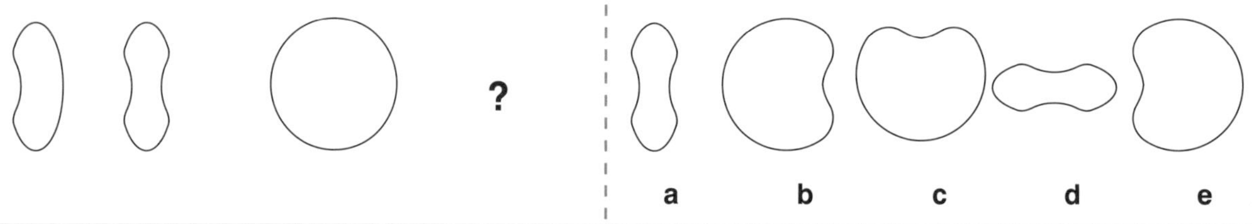

?
a
b
c
d
e

YOU NOW HAVE SIX MINUTES TO COMPLETE THE REST OF SECTION 1

1

?
a
b
c
d
e

2

?
a
b
c
d
e

3

?
a
b
c
d
e

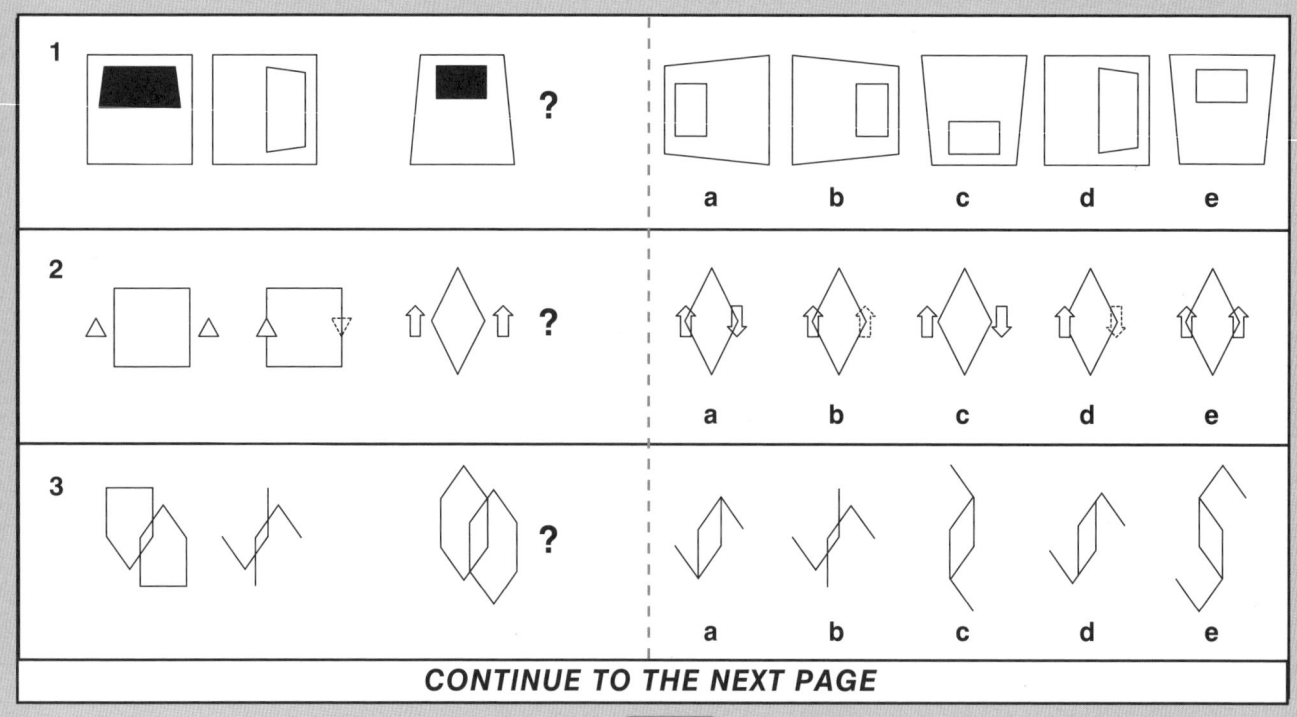

CONTINUE TO THE NEXT PAGE

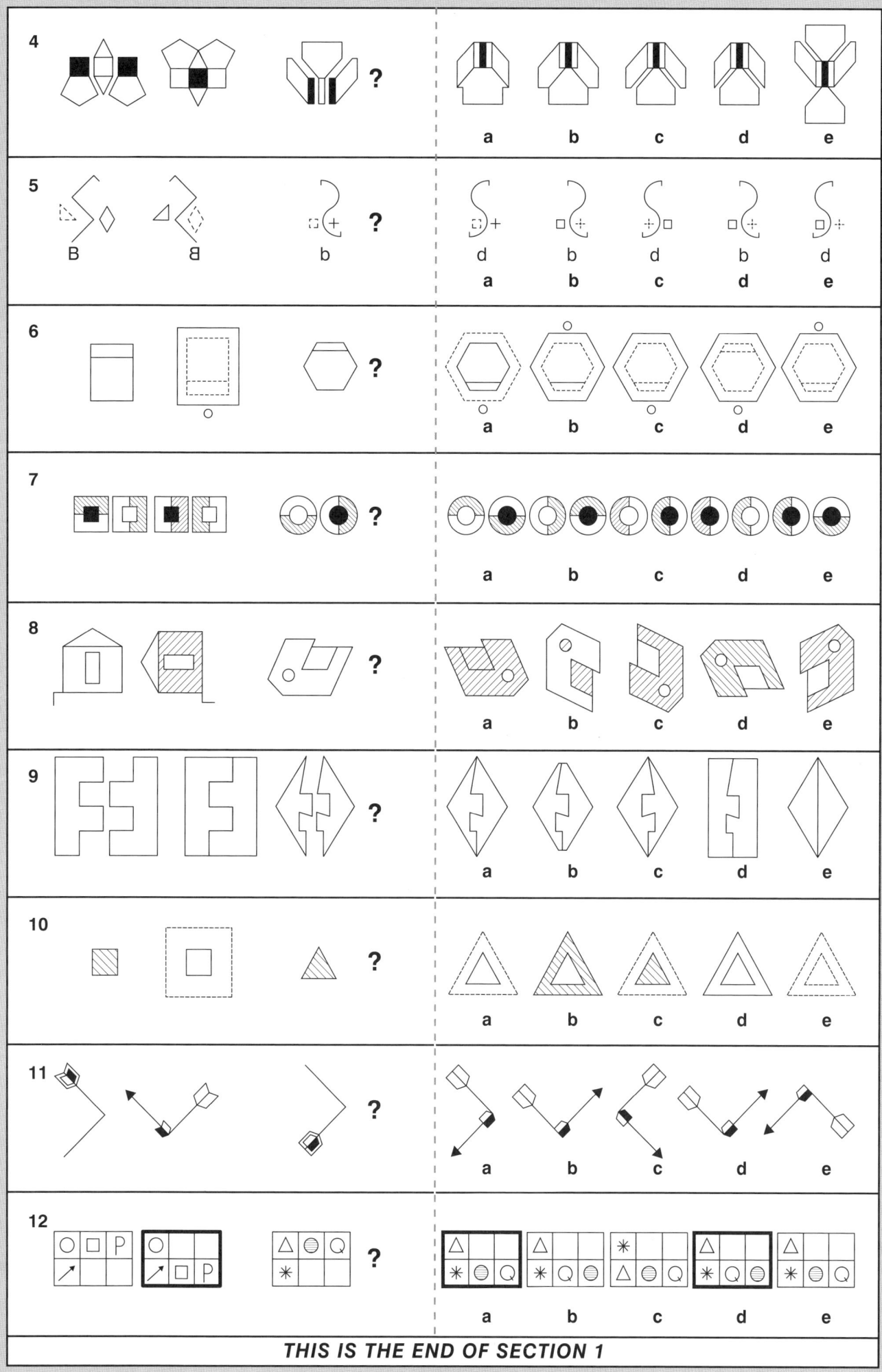

Section 2

Which is the odd one out?

Example

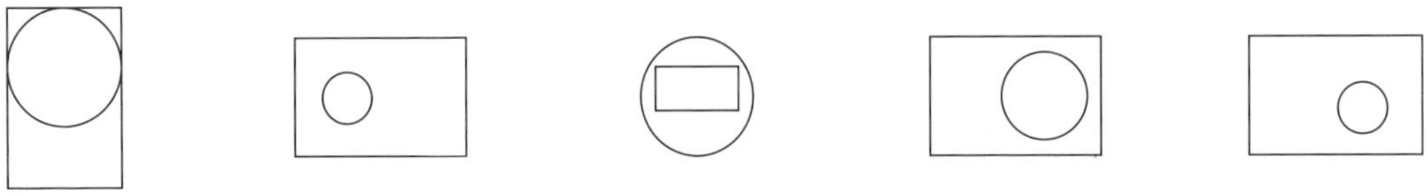

a b c d e

Practice 1

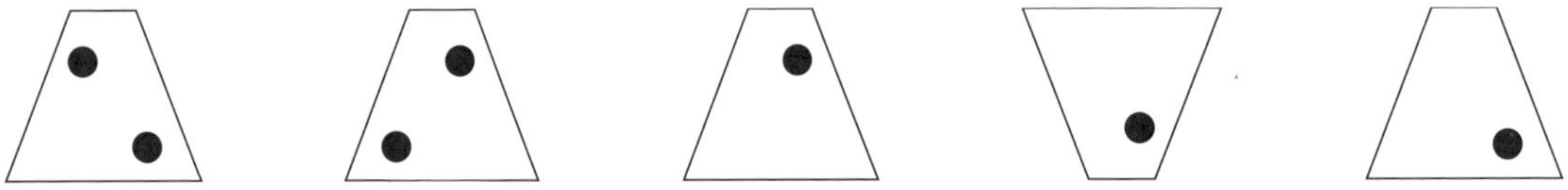

a b c d e

Practice 2

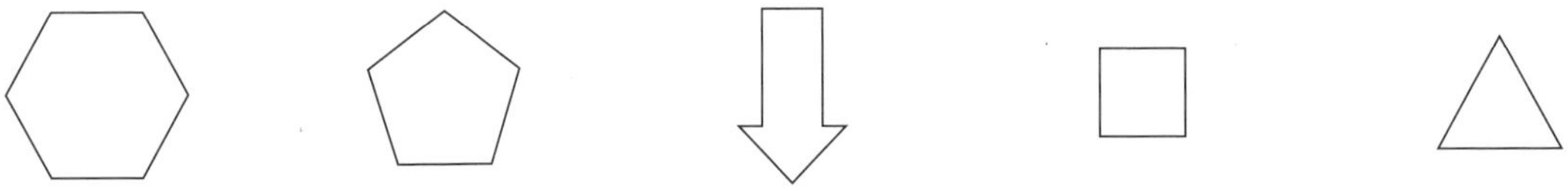

a b c d e

YOU NOW HAVE SIX MINUTES TO COMPLETE THE REST OF SECTION 2

1

a b c d e

2

a b c d e

3

a b c d e

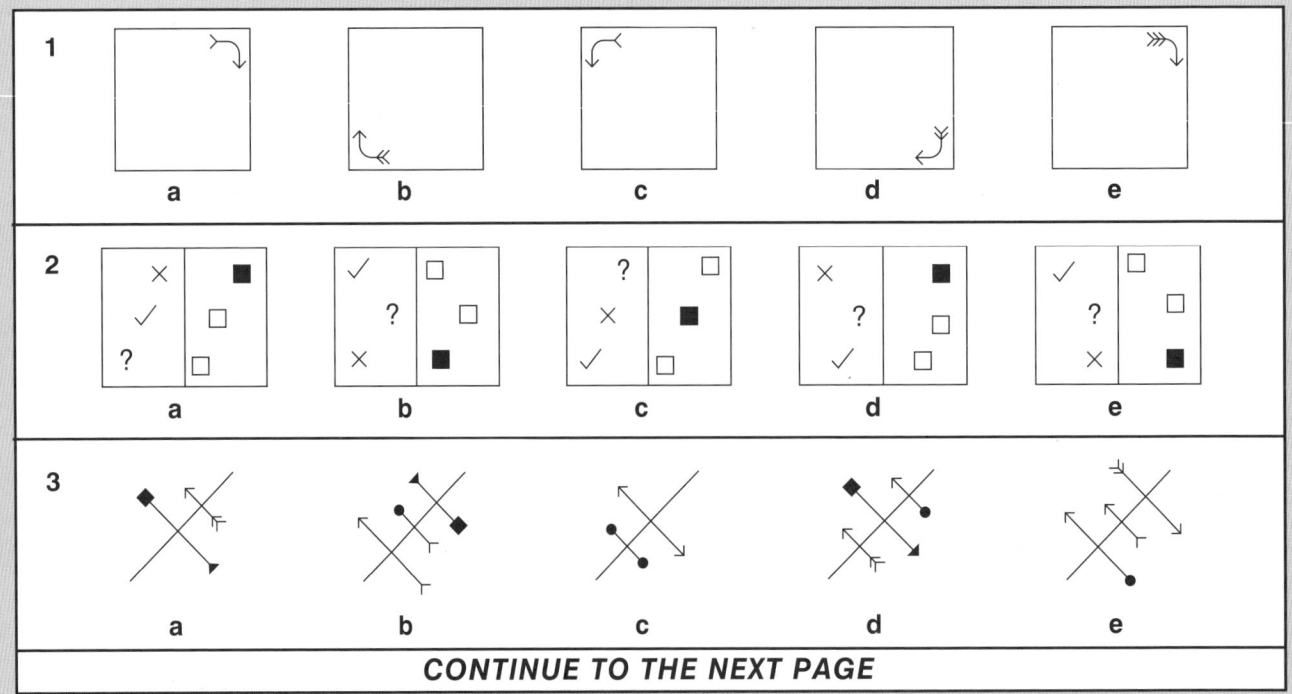

CONTINUE TO THE NEXT PAGE

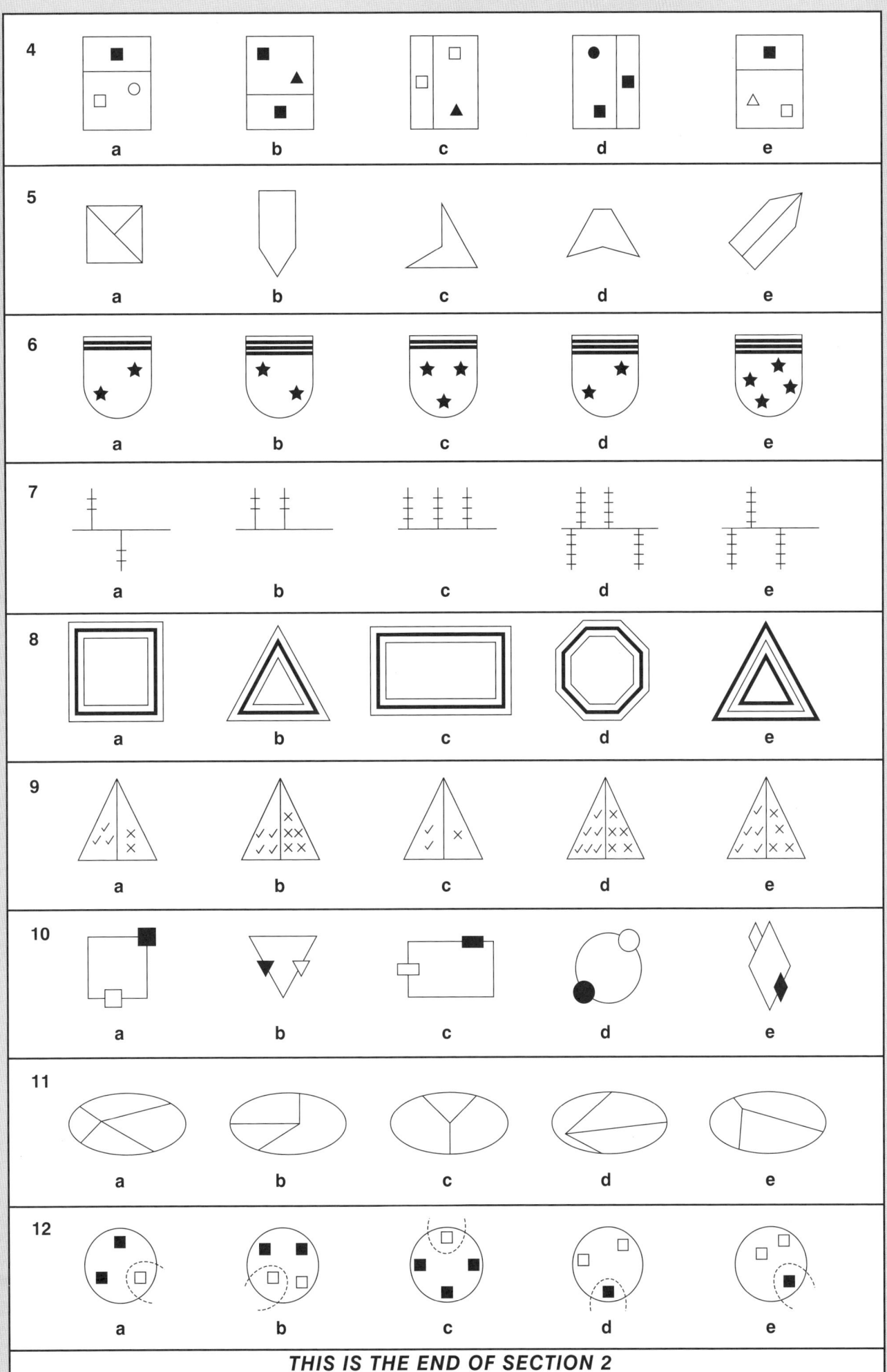

Section 3

Which one comes next?

Example

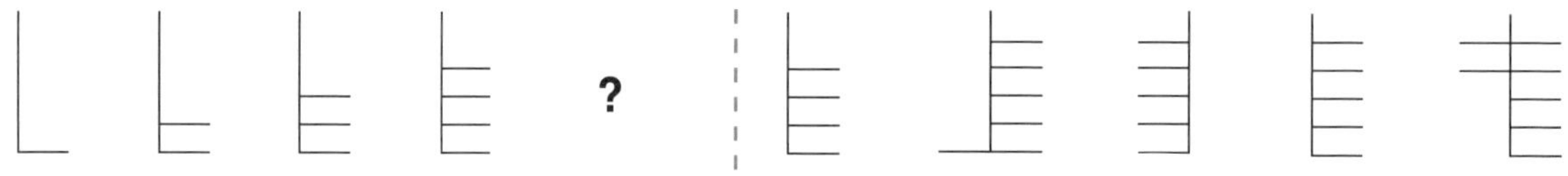

a b c (d) e

Practice 1

a b c d e

Practice 2

a b c d e

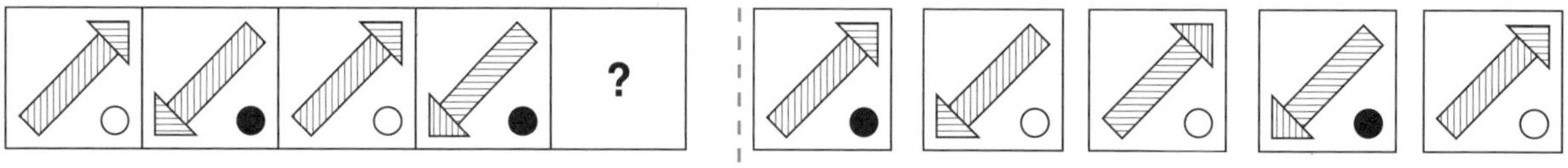

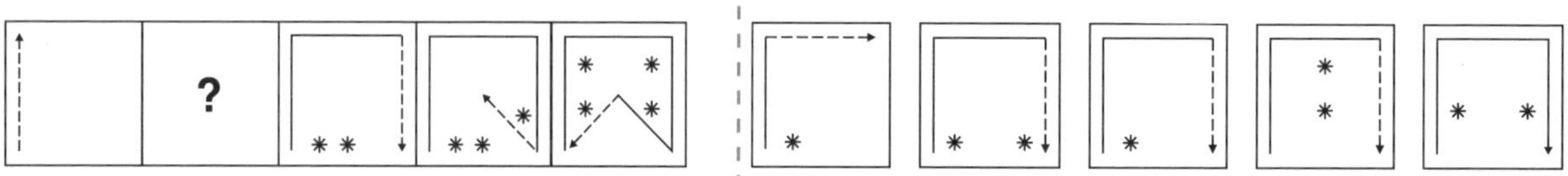

YOU NOW HAVE SIX MINUTES TO COMPLETE THE REST OF SECTION 3

1

a b c d e

2

a b c d e

3

a b c d e

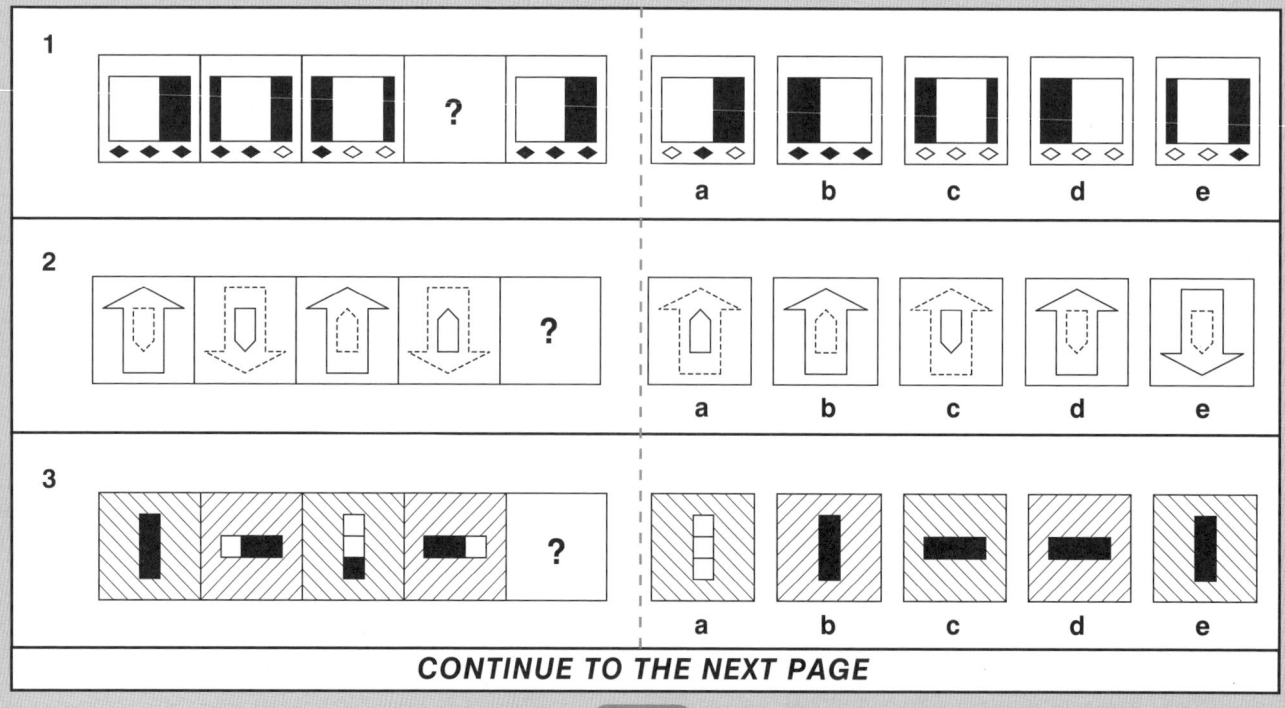

CONTINUE TO THE NEXT PAGE

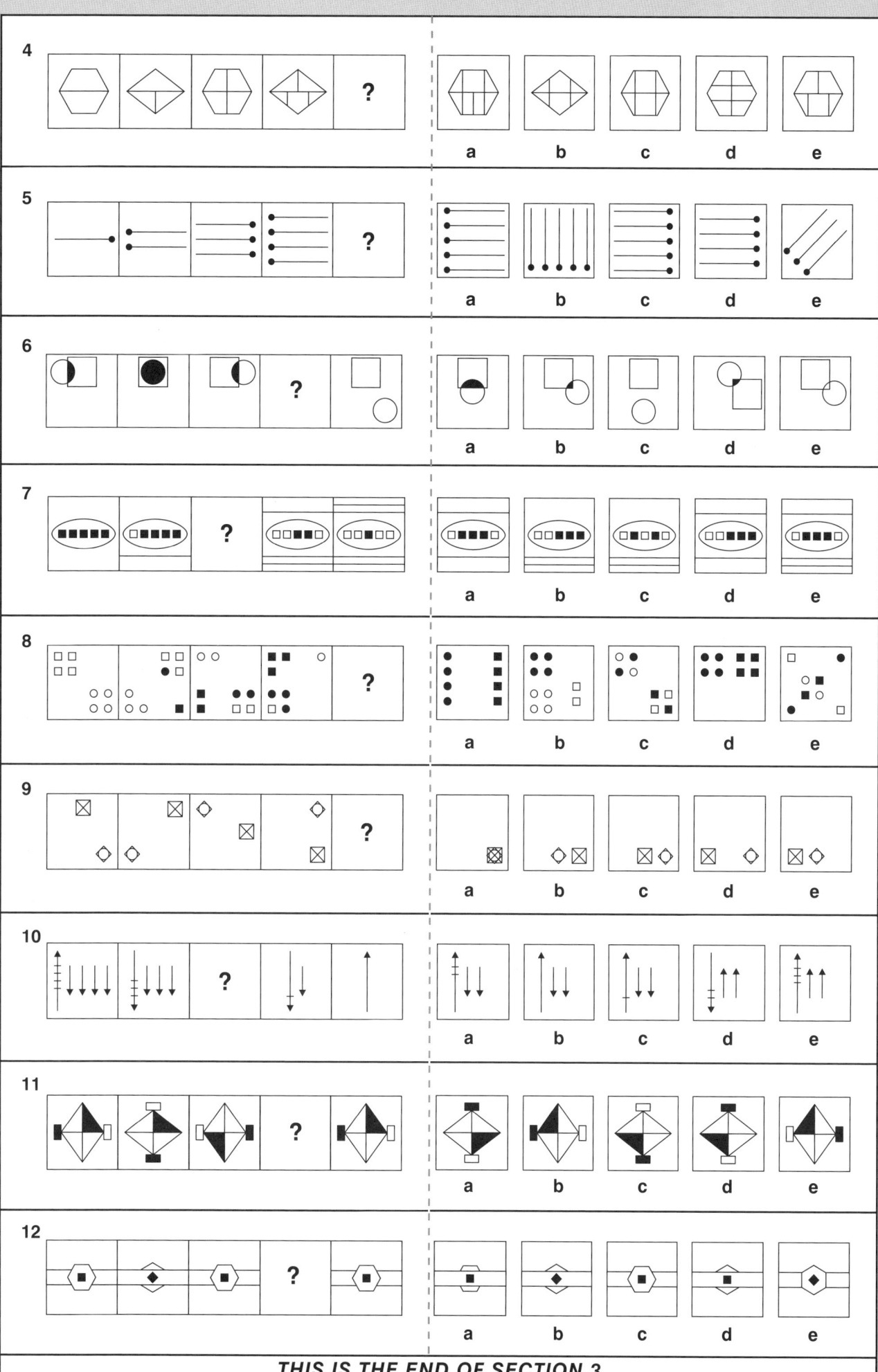

Section 4

Which code matches the shape or pattern given at the end of each line?

Example

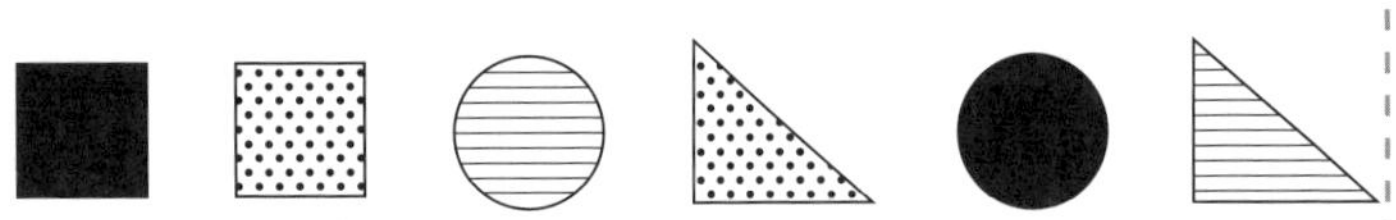

						BZ	AZ	CX	BY	CZ
AX	AY	BZ	CY	BX	?	a	b	c	d	(e)

Practice 1

				RY	SX	RS	SY	RX
RX	SX	RY	?	a	b	c	d	e

Practice 2

				QE	PF	QF	PE	PG
PE	PF	QG	?	a	b	c	d	e

YOU NOW HAVE SIX MINUTES TO COMPLETE THE REST OF SECTION 4

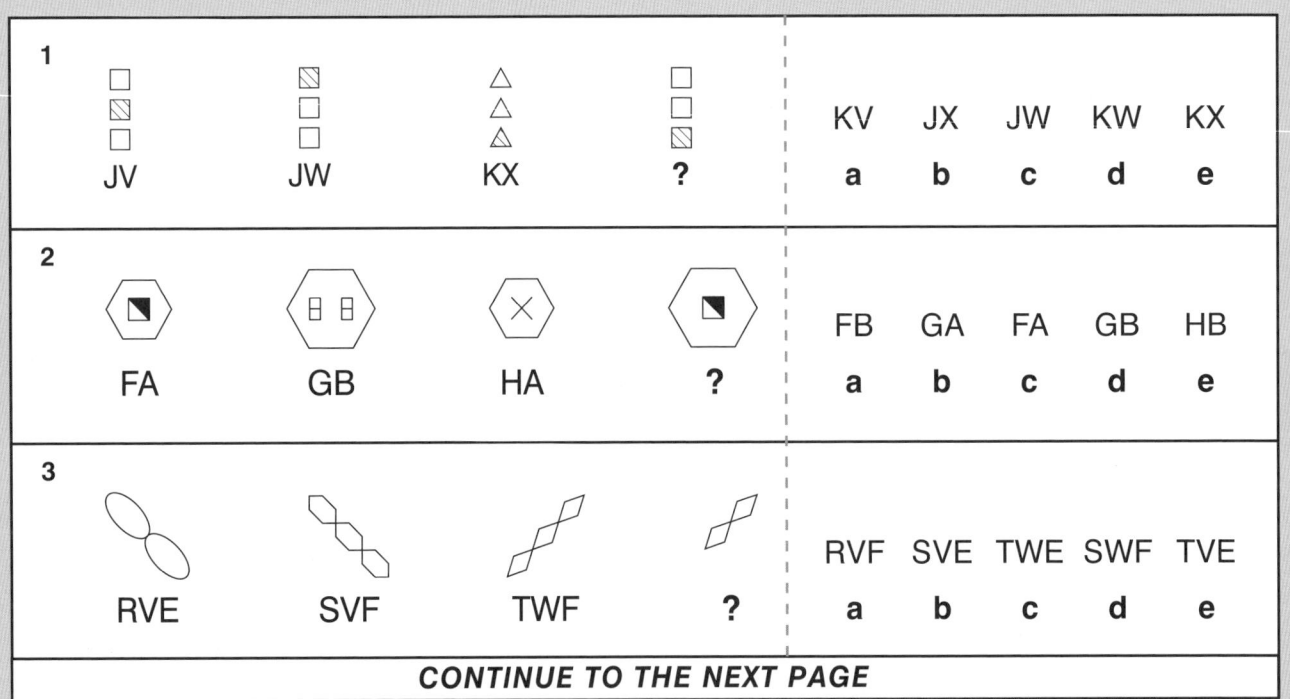

CONTINUE TO THE NEXT PAGE

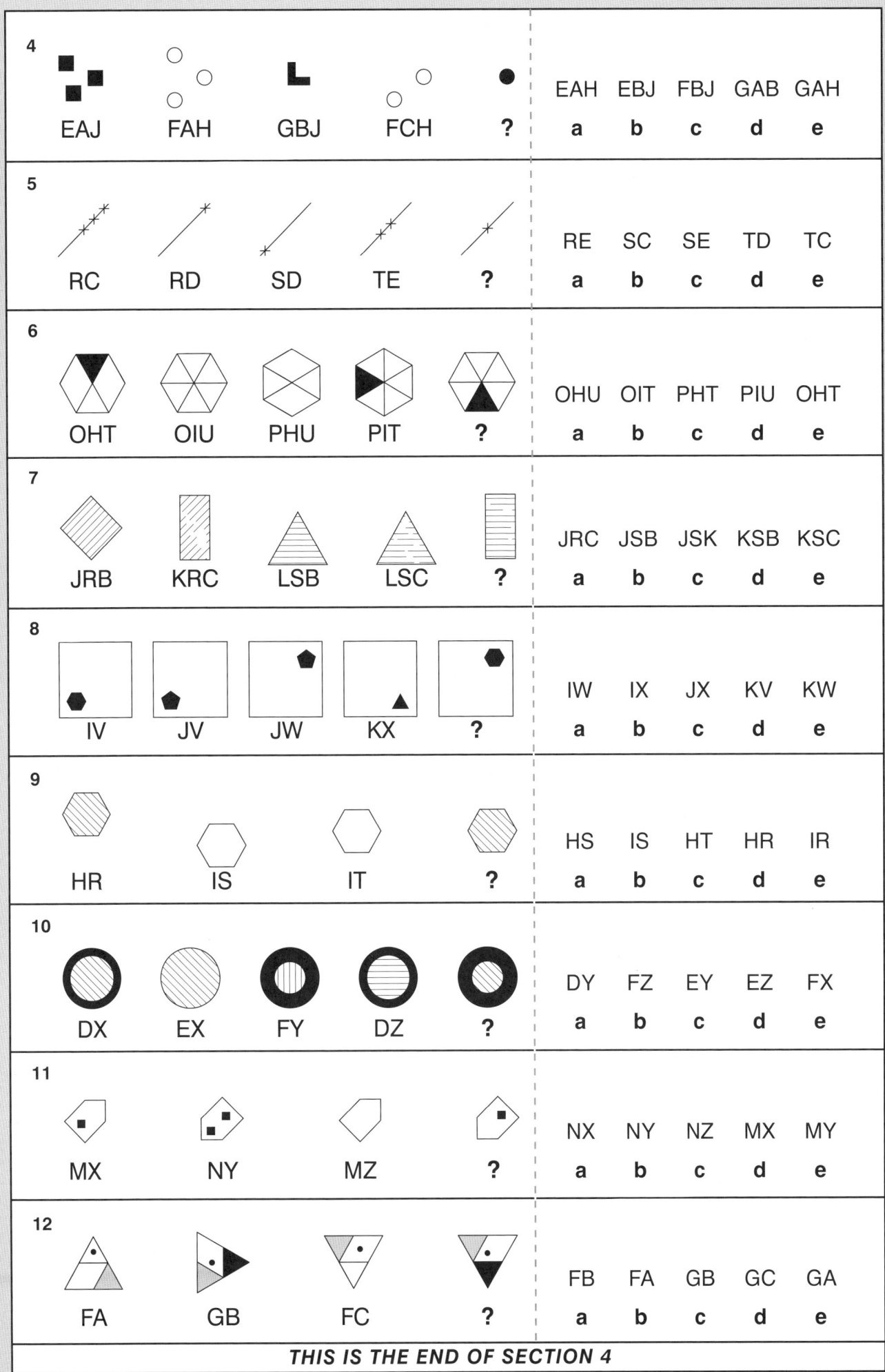

Section 5

Which shape or pattern completes the larger square?

Example

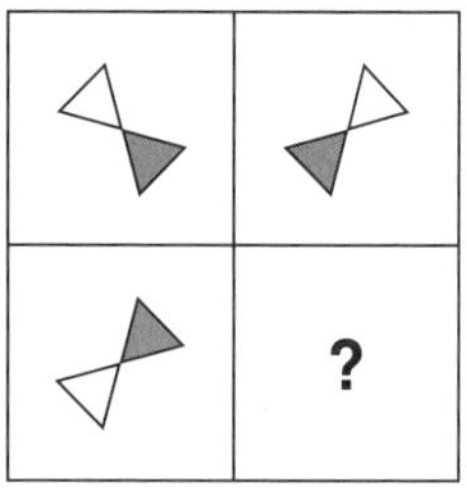

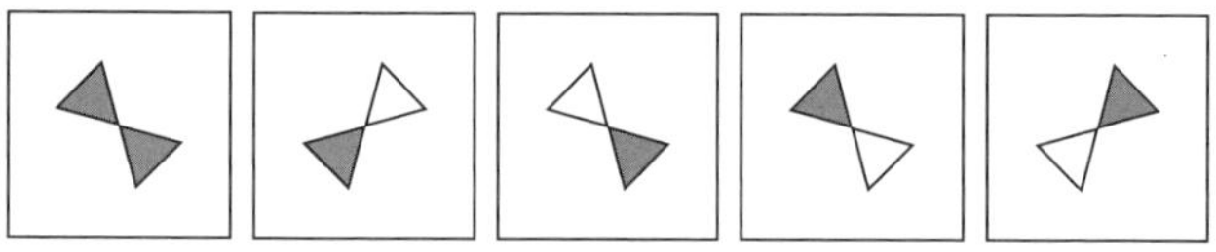

a b c d e

Practice 1

a b c d e

Practice 2

a b c d e

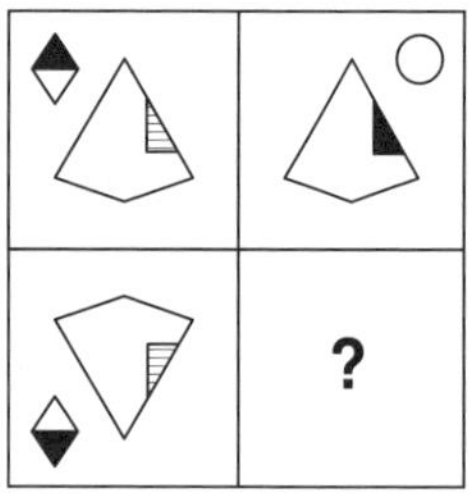

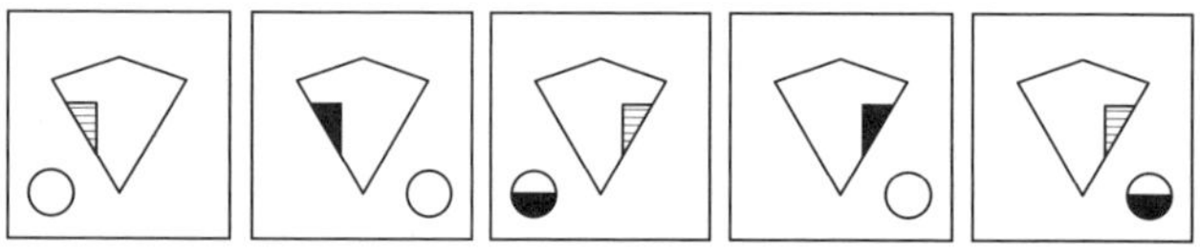

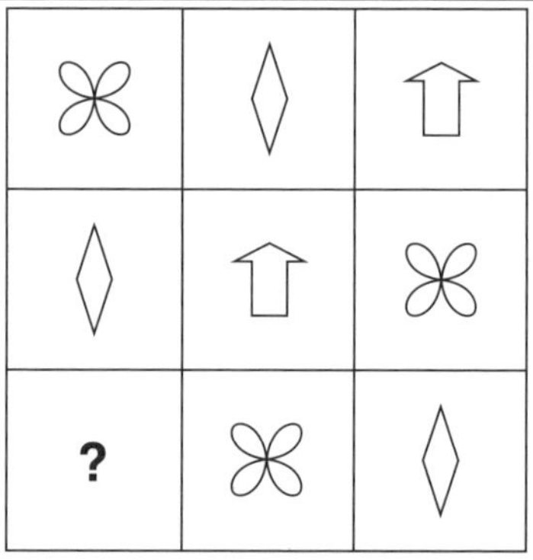

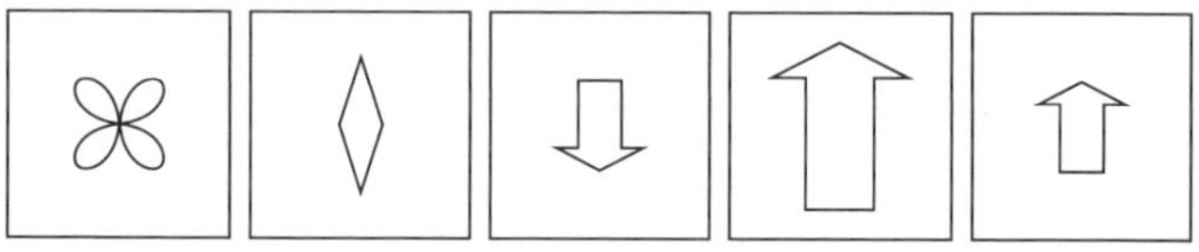

YOU NOW HAVE SIX MINUTES TO COMPLETE THE REST OF SECTION 5

1

a b c d e

2

a b c d e

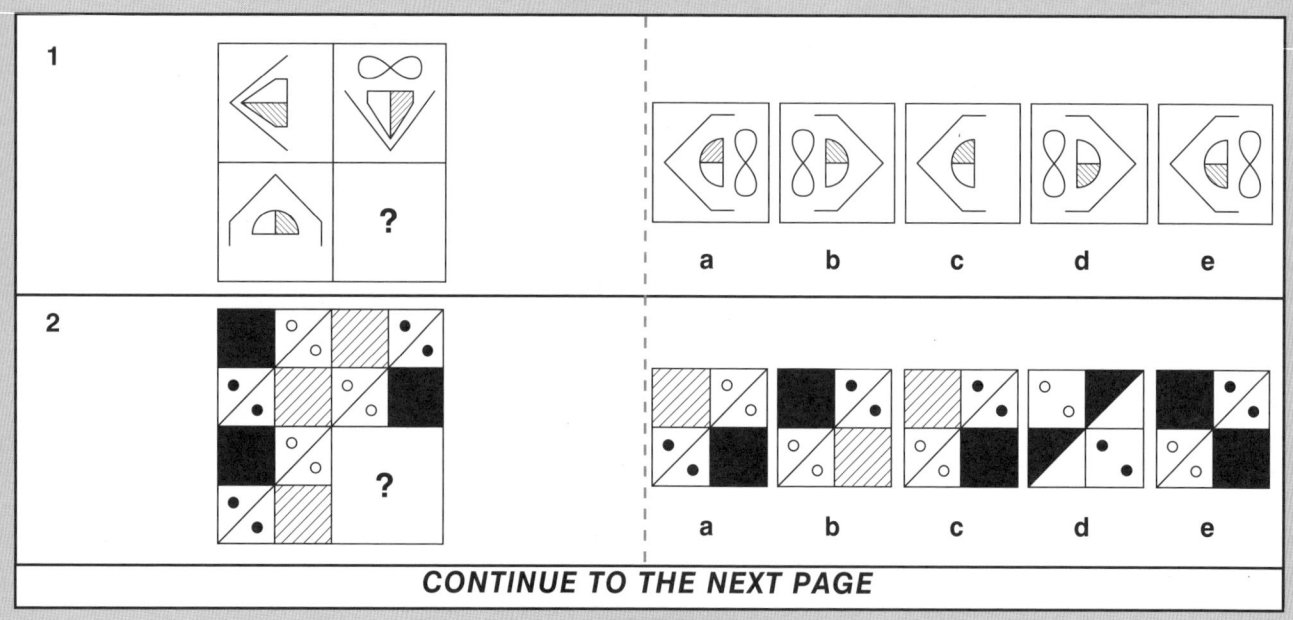

CONTINUE TO THE NEXT PAGE

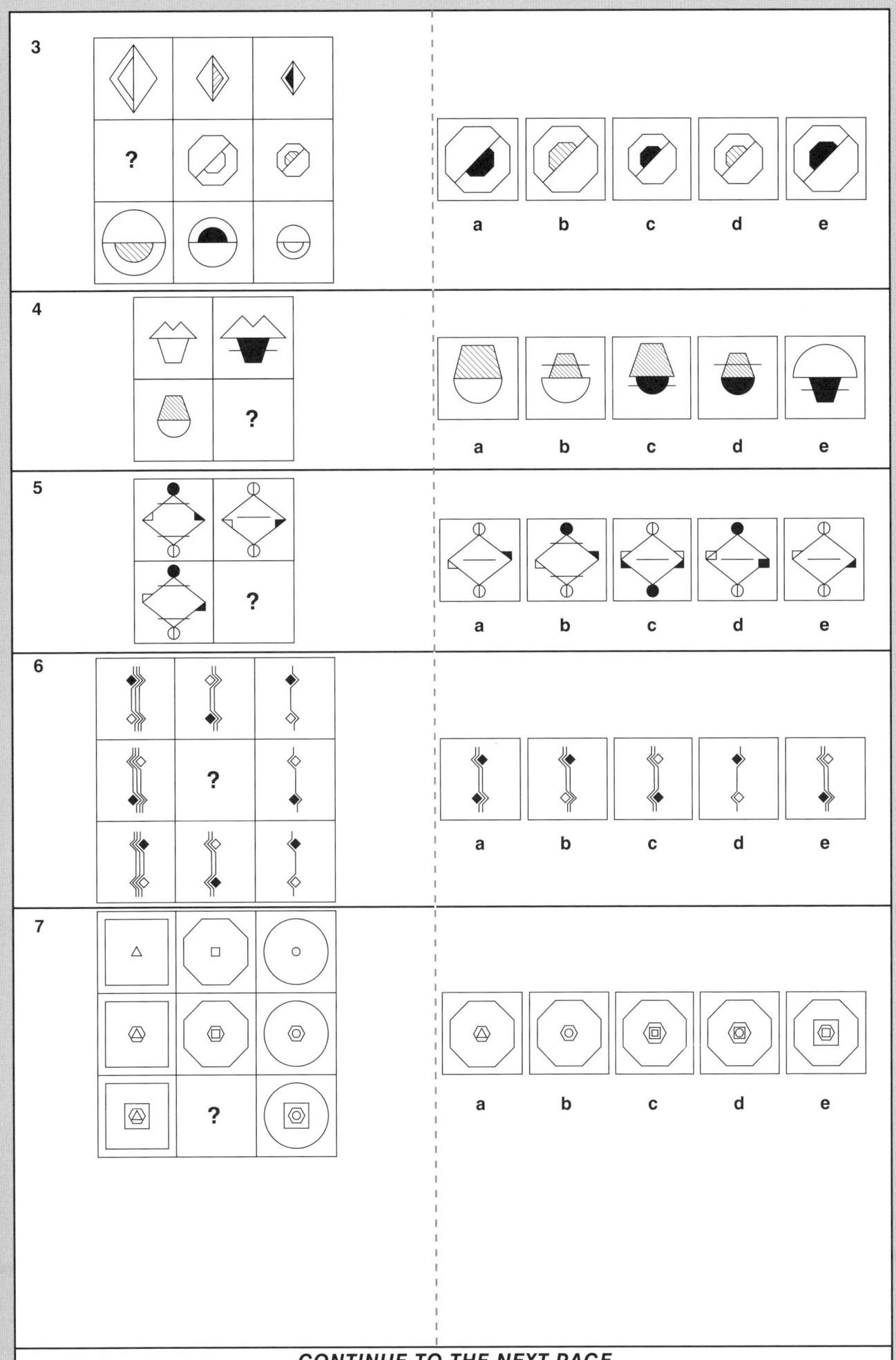

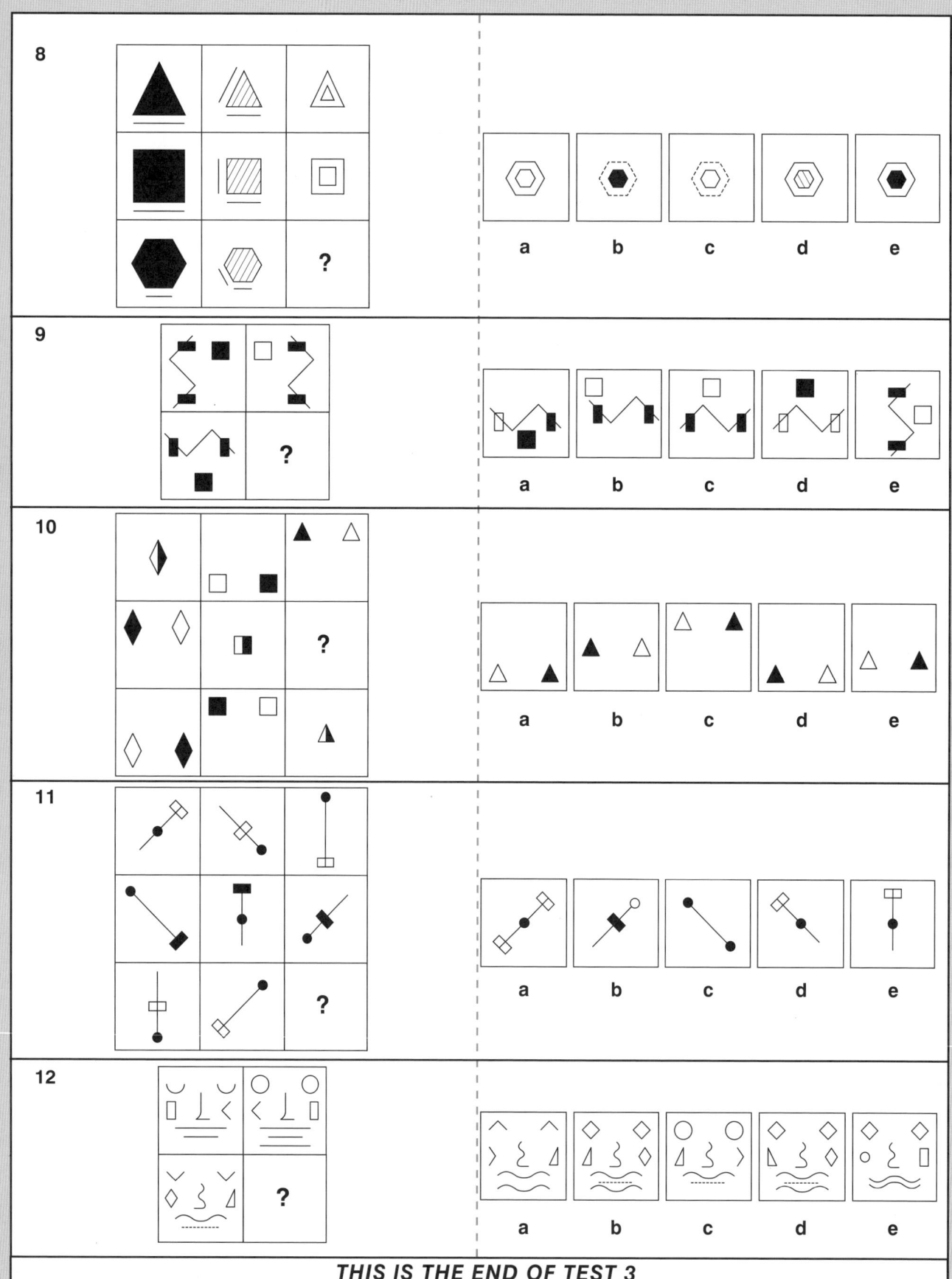

11+
Non-verbal Reasoning

Multiple-choice Test Papers
Pack 1
Test 4

Read the following:

- Do not begin the test or open this booklet until told to do so. Follow the instructions for sitting the test
- Work as quickly and as carefully as you can
- Answers should be marked in the answer booklet provided, not in this test booklet
- You may do rough working on a separate sheet of paper
- Be careful to keep your place in the accompanying answer booklet
- You will have 30 minutes to complete the test

OXFORD
UNIVERSITY PRESS

Great Clarendon Street, Oxford, OX2 6DP, United Kingdom

Oxford University Press is a department of the University of Oxford. It furthers the University's objective of excellence in research, scholarship, and education by publishing worldwide. Oxford is a registered trade mark of Oxford University Press in the UK and in certain other countries

Text © Andrew Baines 2015
Illustrations © Oxford University Press 2015

The moral rights of the authors have been asserted

First published in 2015

All rights reserved. No part of this publication may be reproduced, stored in a retrieval system, or transmitted, in any form or by any means, without the prior permission in writing of Oxford University Press, or as expressly permitted by law, by licence or under terms agreed with the appropriate reprographics rights organization. Enquiries concerning reproduction outside the scope of the above should be sent to the Rights Department, Oxford University Press, at the address above.

You must not circulate this work in any other form and you must impose this same condition on any acquirer

British Library Cataloguing in Publication Data
Data available

978-0-19-274087-8

Paper used in the production of this book is a natural, recyclable product made from wood grown in sustainable forests. The manufacturing process conforms to the environmental regulations of the country of origin.

Printed in China

Acknowledgements

The publishers would like to thank the following for permissions to use copyright material:

Cover illustrations: Lo Cole

Although we have made every effort to trace and contact all copyright holders before publication this has not been possible in all cases. If notified, the publisher will rectify any errors or omissions at the earliest opportunity.

Links to third party websites are provided by Oxford in good faith and for information only. Oxford disclaims any responsibility for the materials contained in any third party website referenced in this work.

The manufacturer's authorised representative in the EU for product safety is Oxford University Press España S.A. of El Parque Empresarial San Fernando de Henares, Avenida de Castilla, 2 – 28830 Madrid (www.oup.es/en or product.safety@oup.com). OUP España S.A. also acts as importer into Spain of products made by the manufacturer.

Section 1

Which shape or pattern on the right completes the second pair in the same way as the first pair?

Example

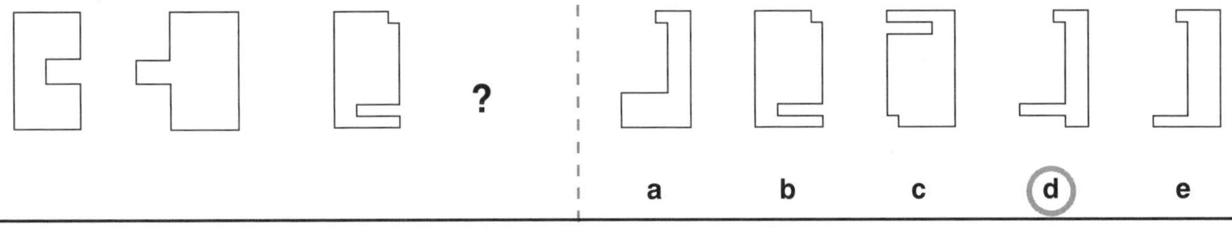

?
a
b
c
d
e

Practice 1

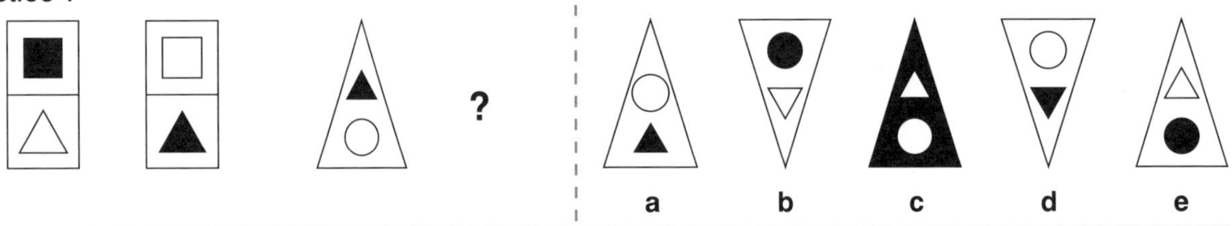

?
a
b
c
d
e

Practice 2

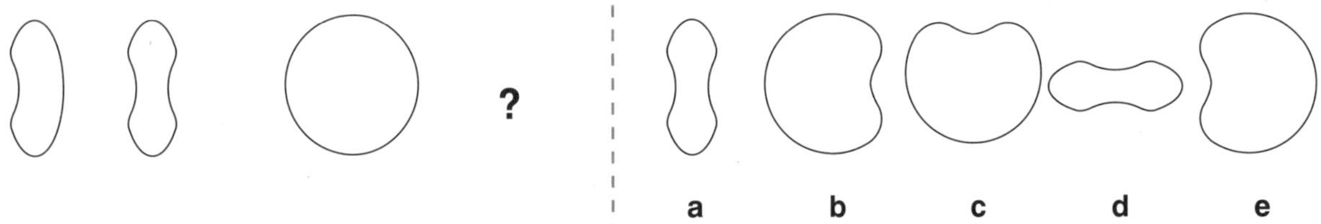

?
a
b
c
d
e

YOU NOW HAVE SIX MINUTES TO COMPLETE THE REST OF SECTION 1

1

?
a
b
c
d
e

2

?
a
b
c
d
e

3

?
a
b
c
d
e

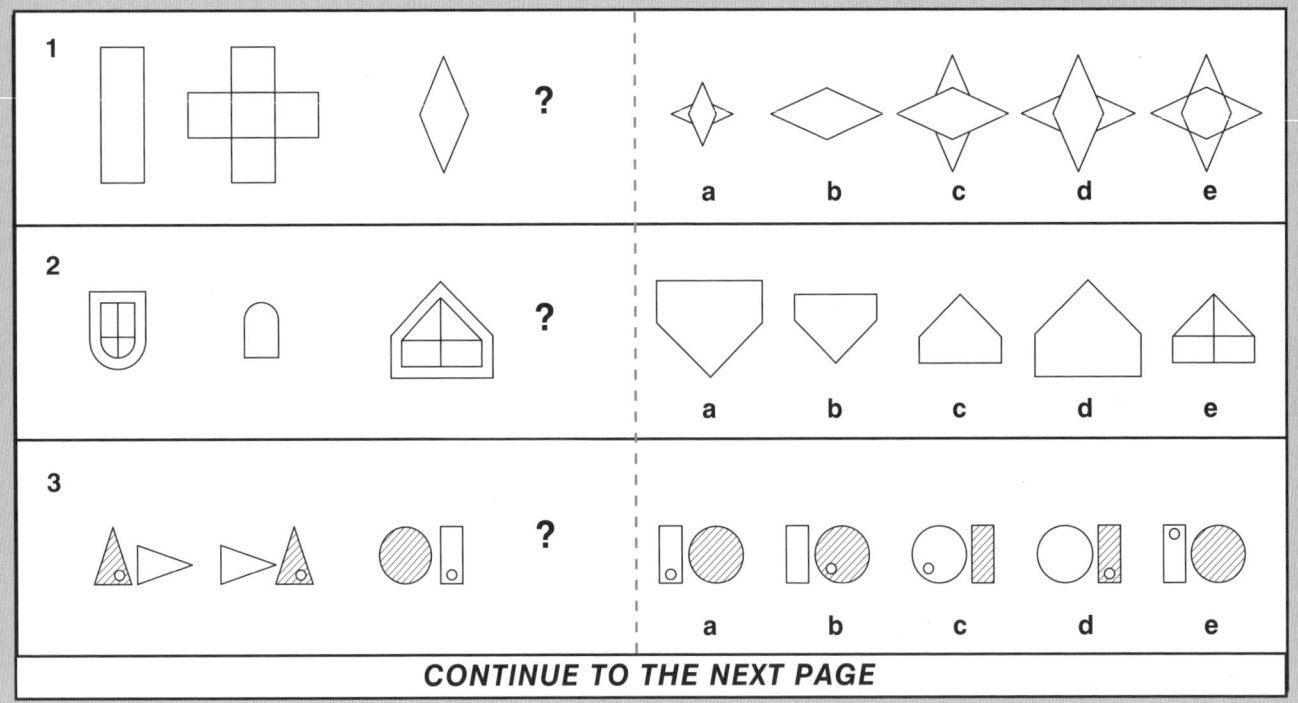

CONTINUE TO THE NEXT PAGE

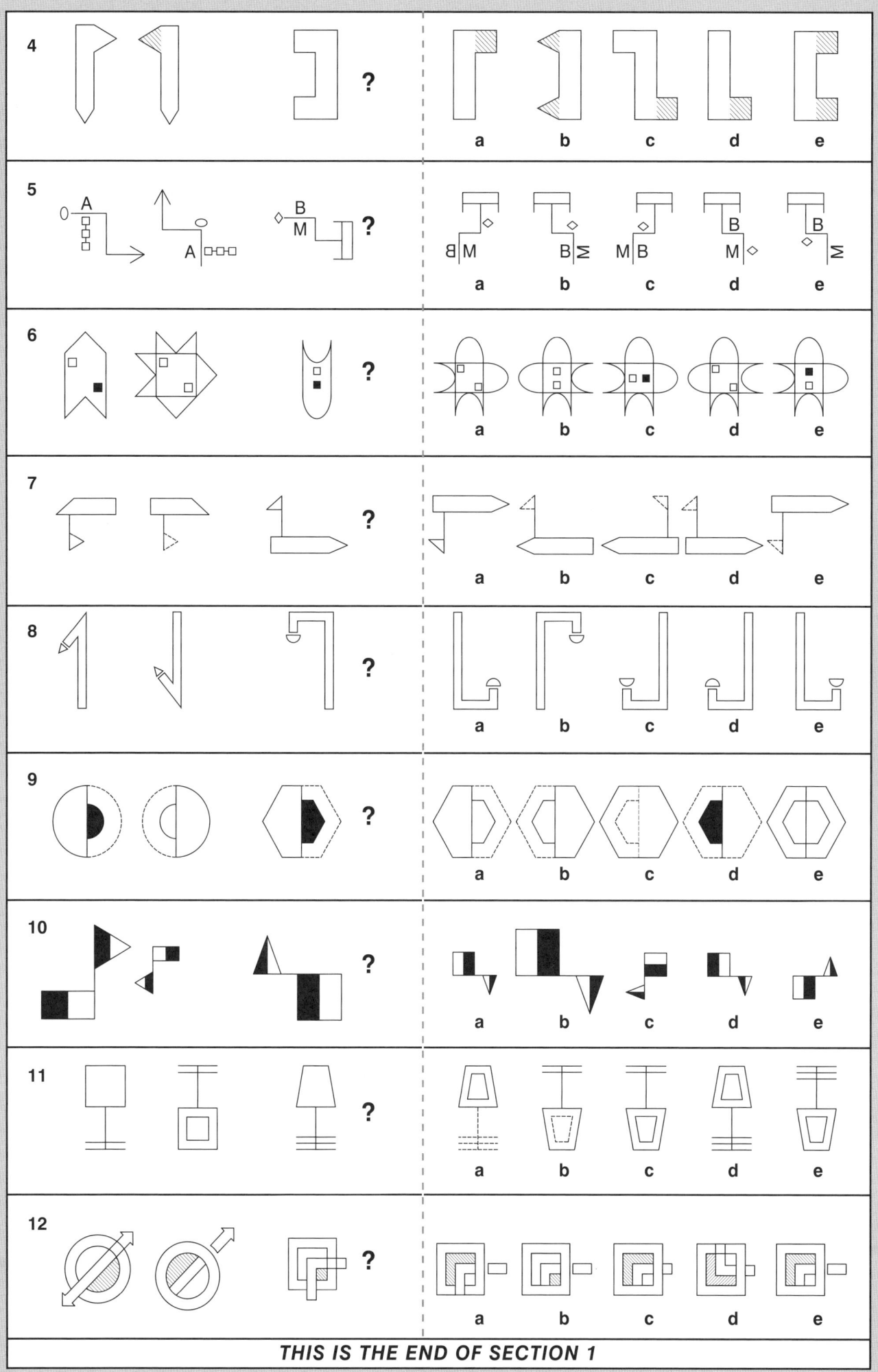

Section 2

Which is the odd one out?

Example

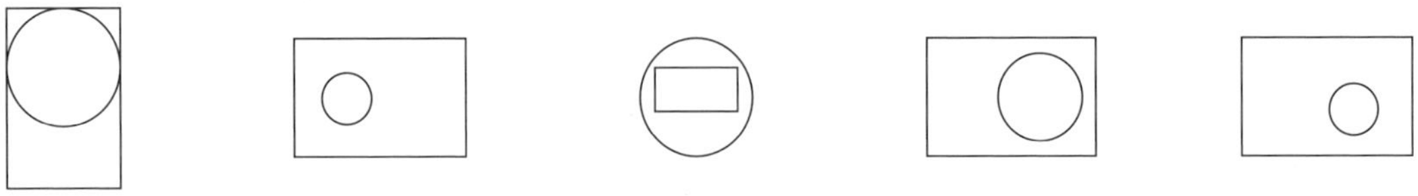

a b c d e

Practice 1

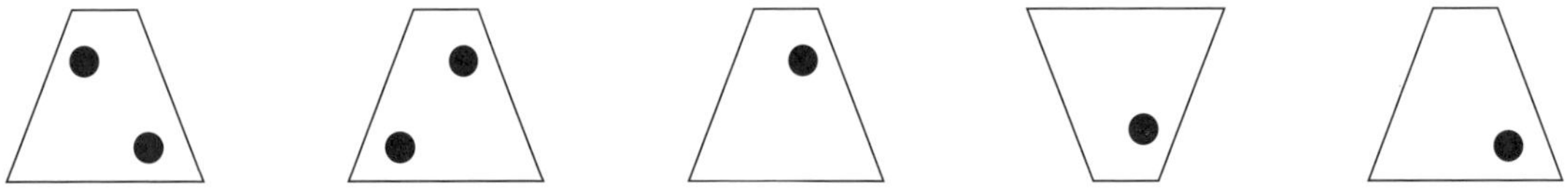

a b c d e

Practice 2

a b c d e

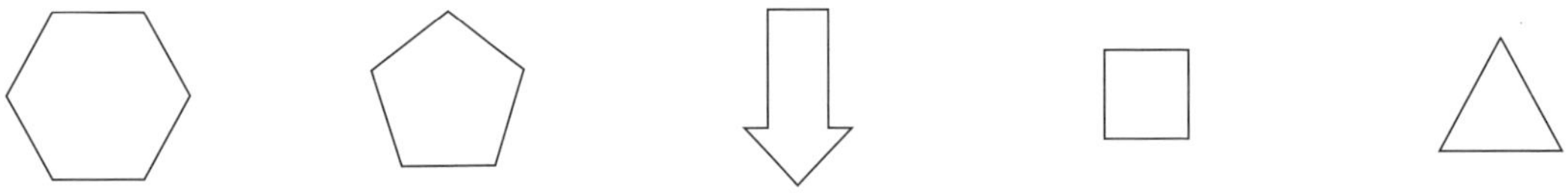

YOU NOW HAVE SIX MINUTES TO COMPLETE THE REST OF SECTION 2

1

a b c d e

2

a b c d e

3

a b c d e

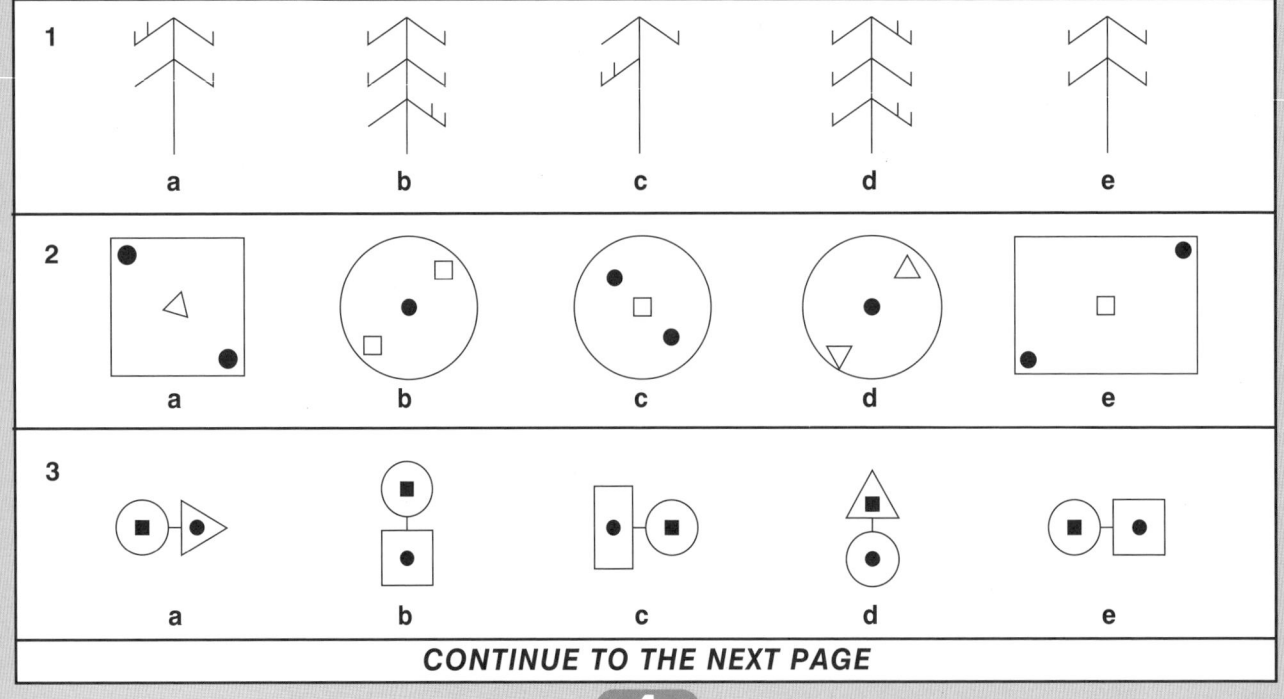

CONTINUE TO THE NEXT PAGE

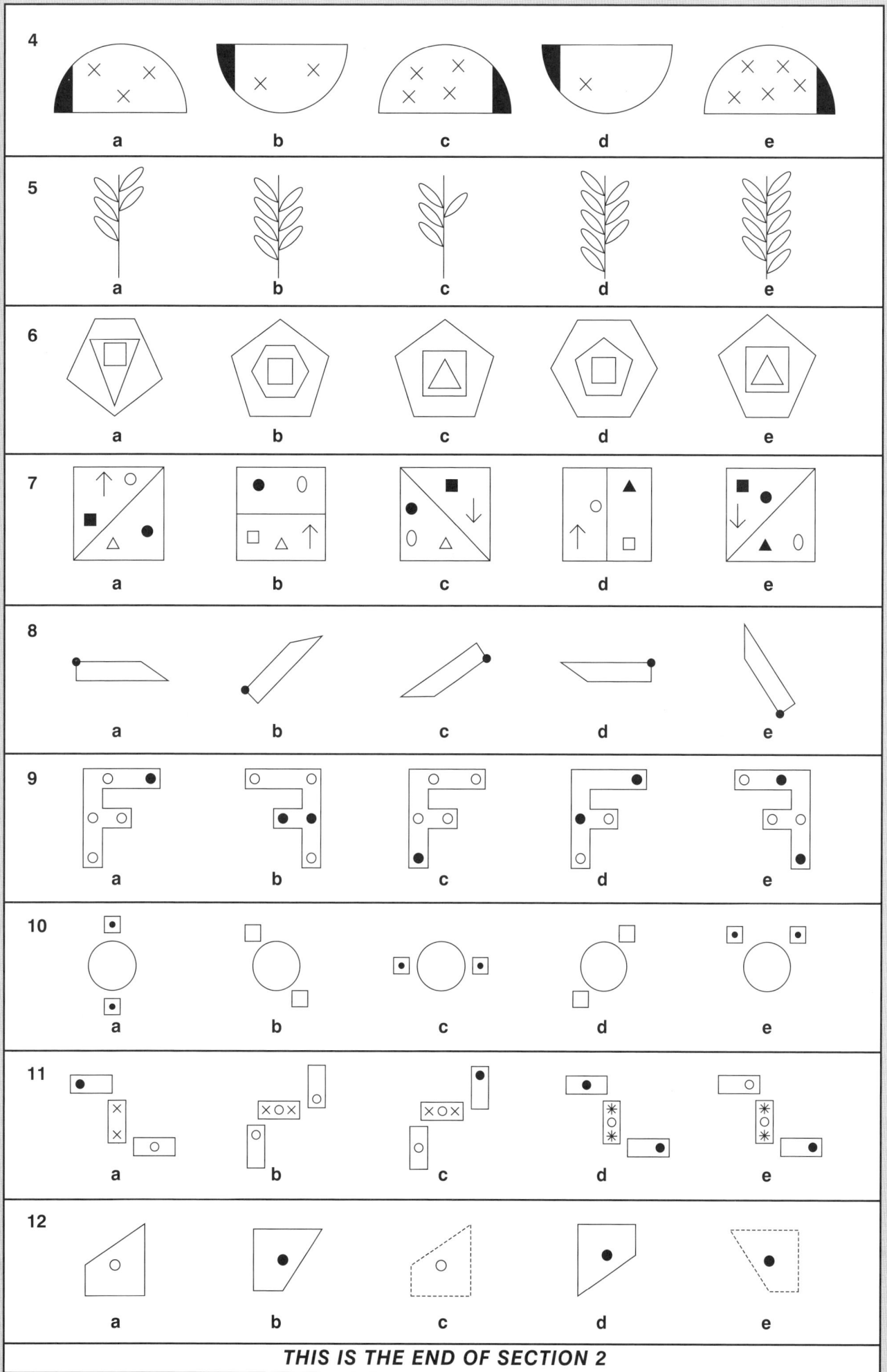

Section 3

Which one comes next?

Example

a b c (d) e

Practice 1

a b c d e

Practice 2

a b c d e

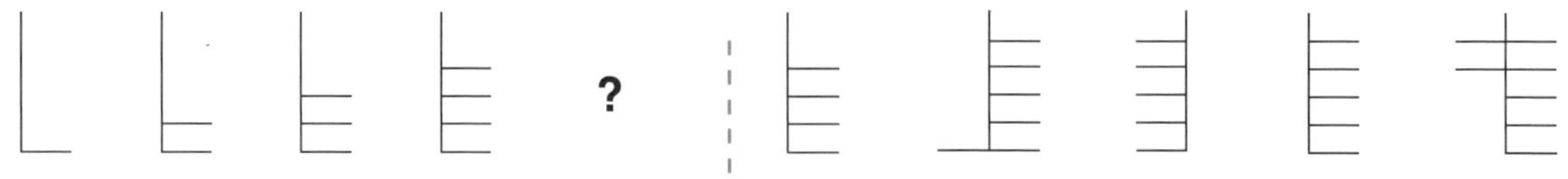

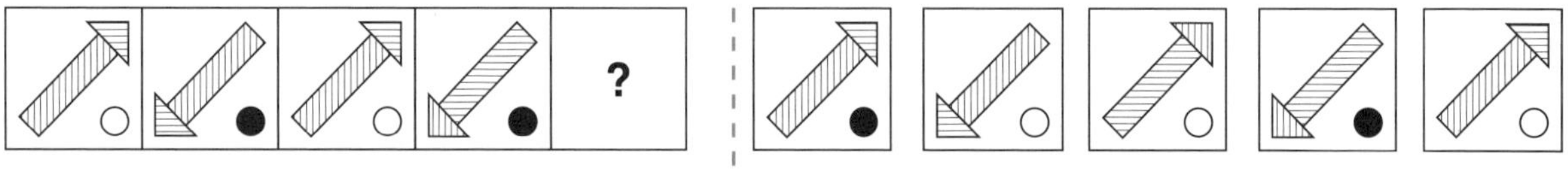

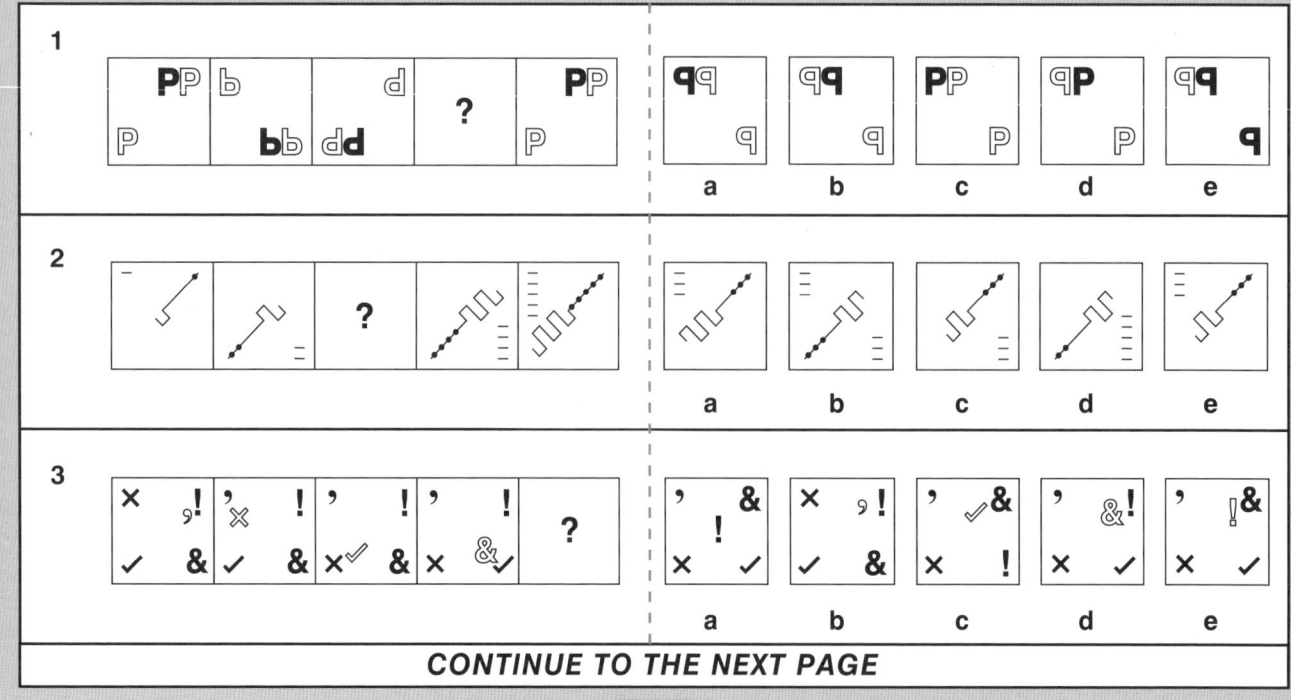

YOU NOW HAVE SIX MINUTES TO COMPLETE THE REST OF SECTION 3

1

a b c d e

2

a b c d e

3

a b c d e

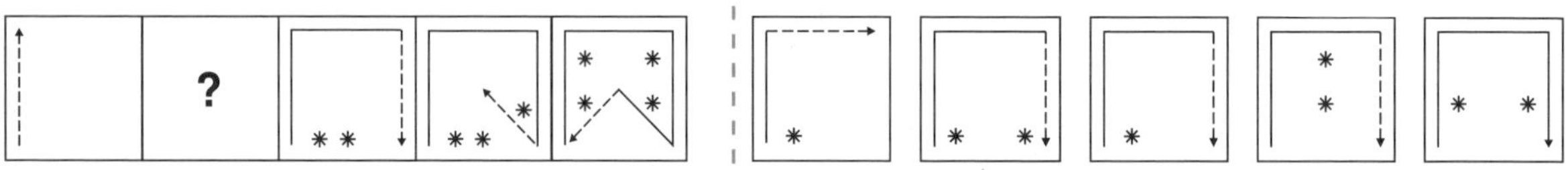

CONTINUE TO THE NEXT PAGE

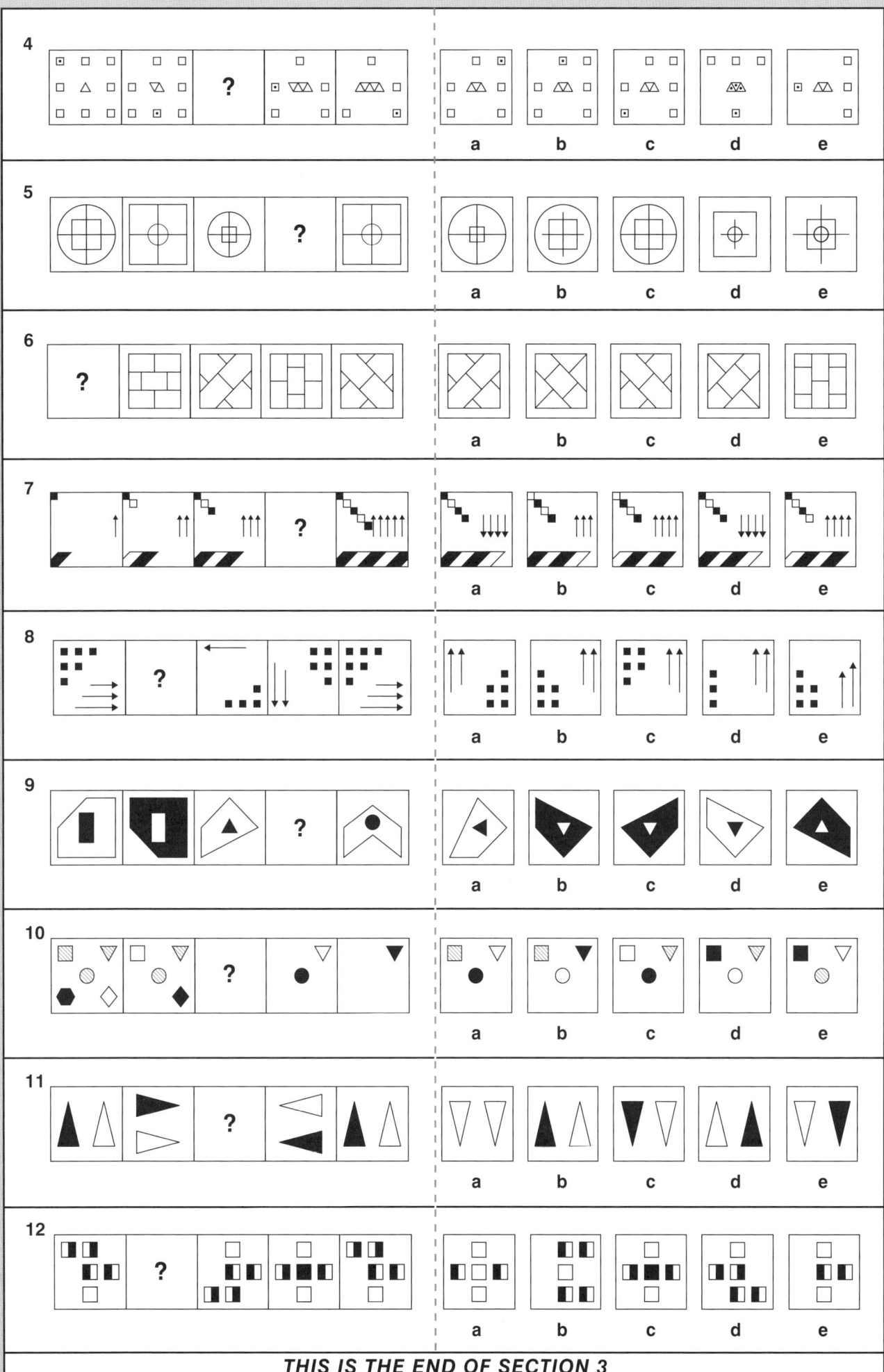

Section 4

Which code matches the shape or pattern given at the end of each line?

Example

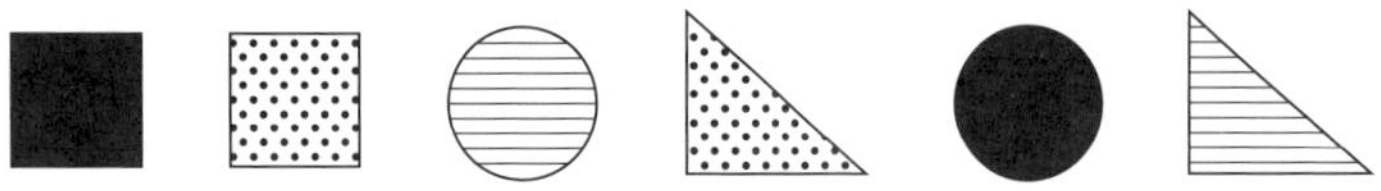

						BZ	AZ	CX	BY	CZ
AX	AY	BZ	CY	BX	?	a	b	c	d	(e)

Practice 1

				RY	SX	RS	SY	RX
RX	SX	RY	?	a	b	c	d	e

Practice 2

				QE	PF	QF	PE	PG
PE	PF	QG	?	a	b	c	d	e

YOU NOW HAVE SIX MINUTES TO COMPLETE THE REST OF SECTION 4

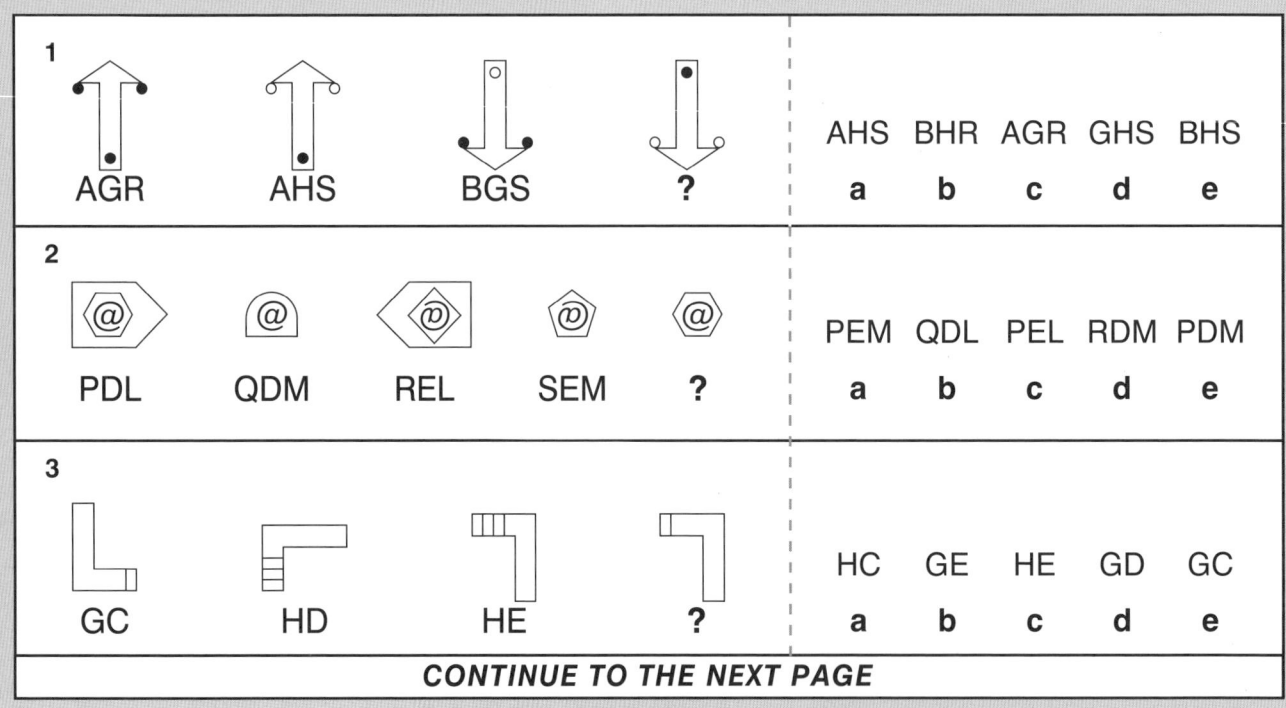

1

				AHS	BHR	AGR	GHS	BHS
AGR	AHS	BGS	?	a	b	c	d	e

2

					PEM	QDL	PEL	RDM	PDM
PDL	QDM	REL	SEM	?	a	b	c	d	e

3

				HC	GE	HE	GD	GC
GC	HD	HE	?	a	b	c	d	e

CONTINUE TO THE NEXT PAGE

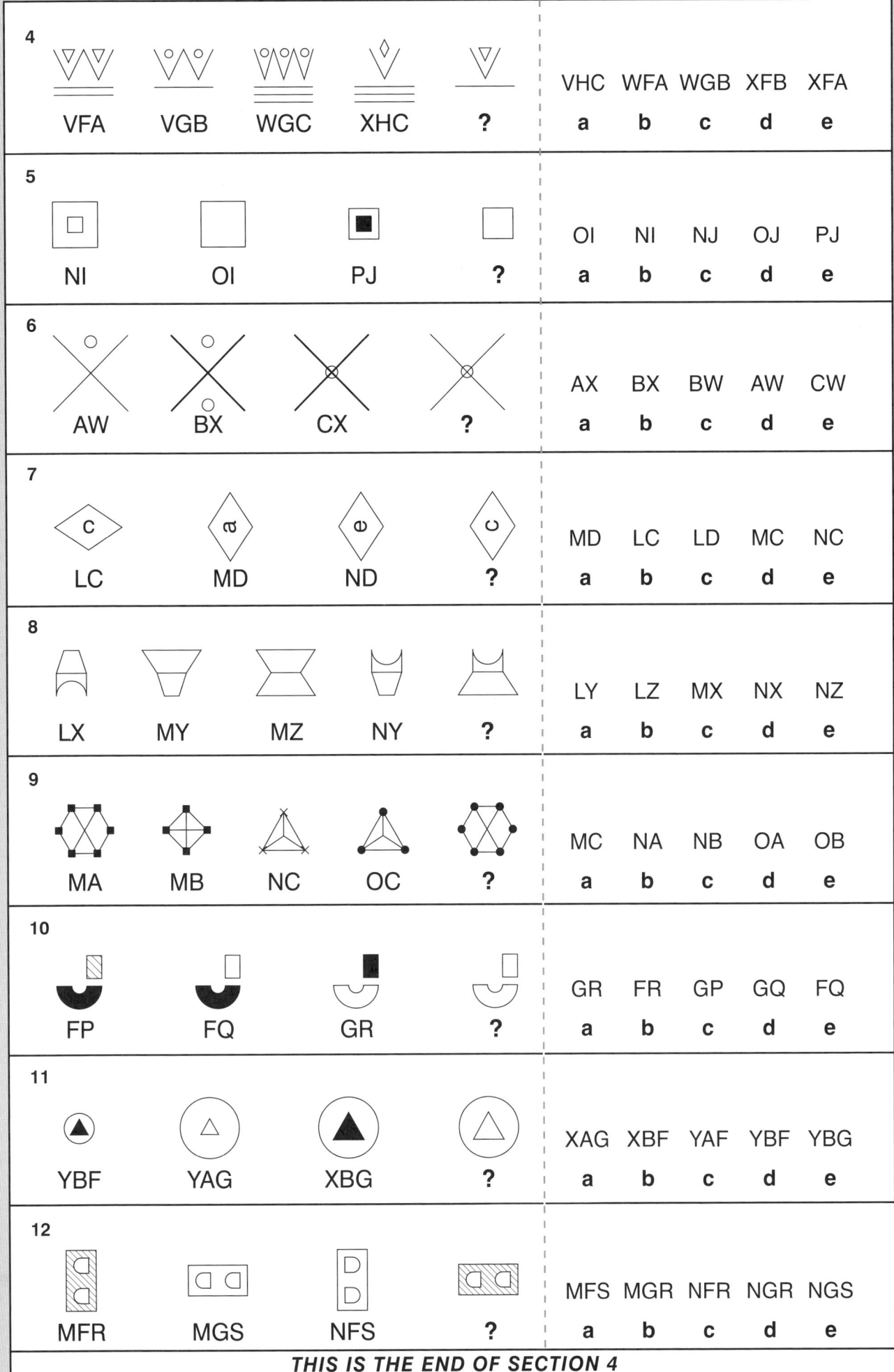

Section 5

Which shape or pattern completes the larger square?

Example

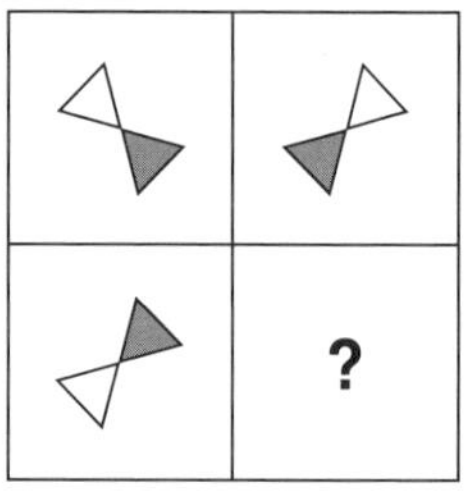

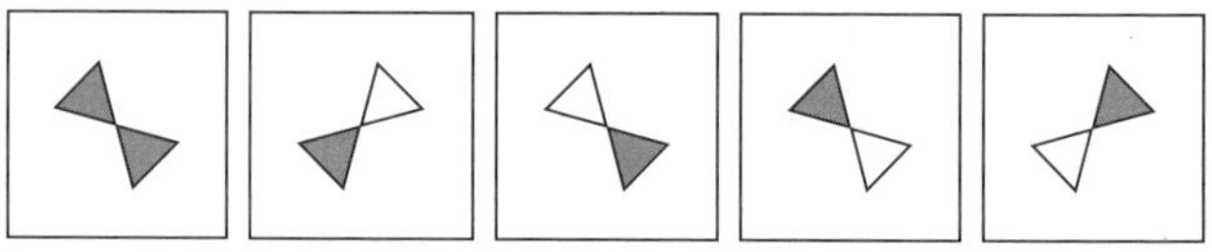

a b c d e

Practice 1

a b c d e

Practice 2

a b c d e

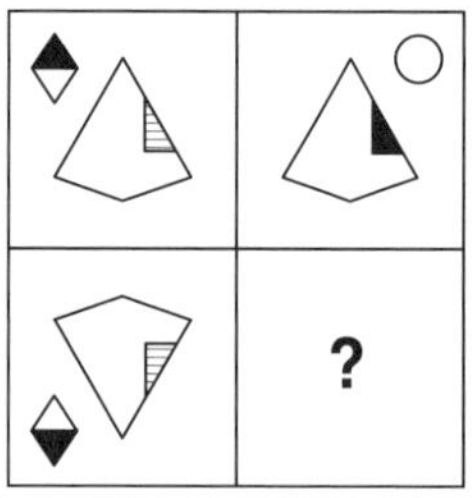

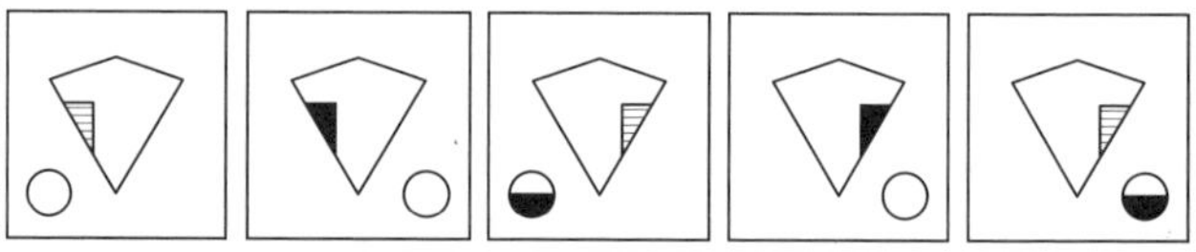

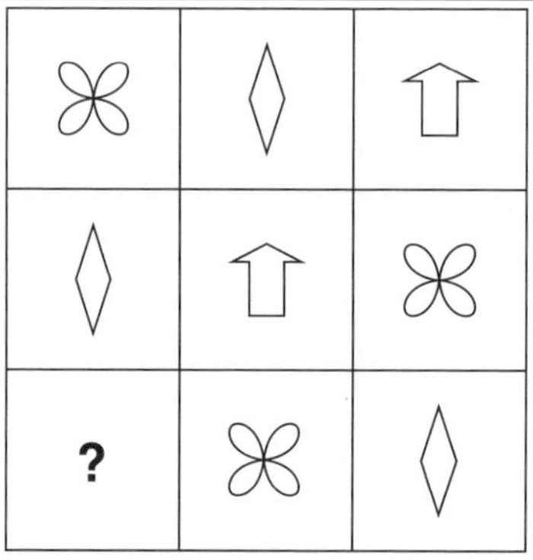

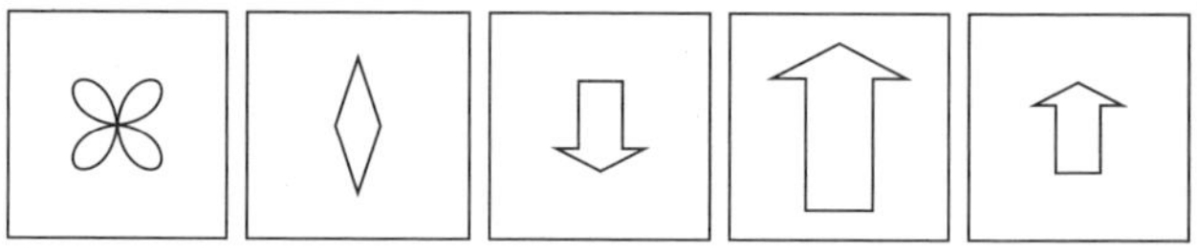

YOU NOW HAVE SIX MINUTES TO COMPLETE THE REST OF SECTION 5

1

a b c d e

2

a b c d e

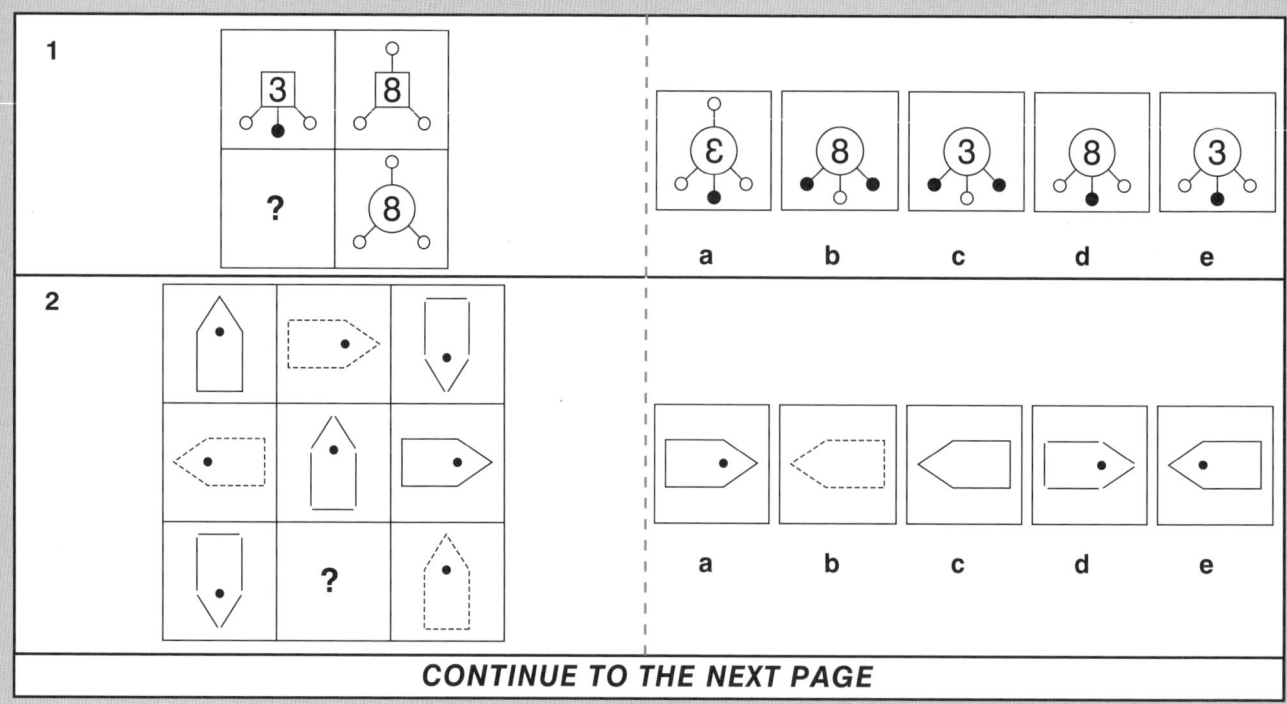

CONTINUE TO THE NEXT PAGE

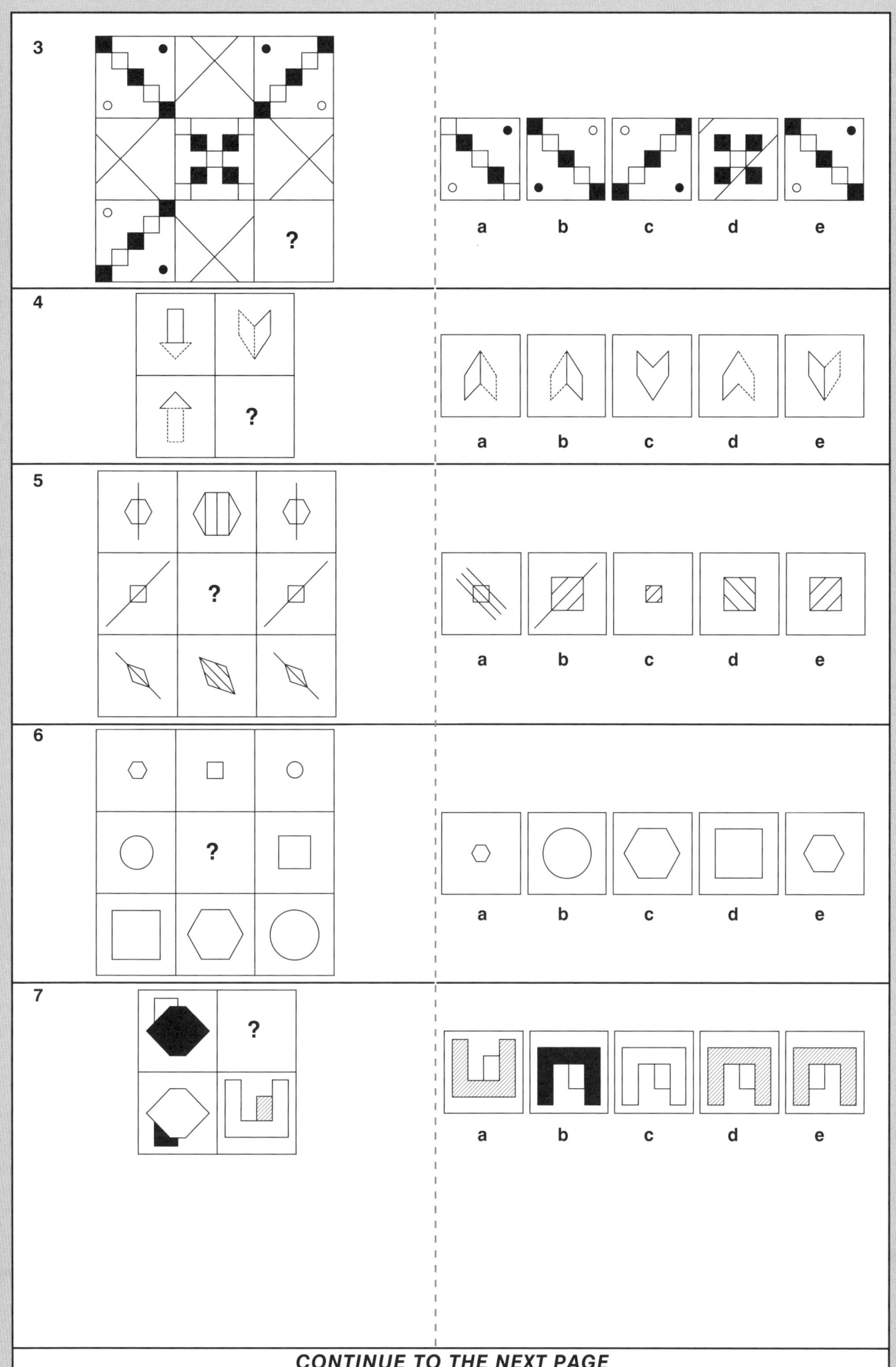

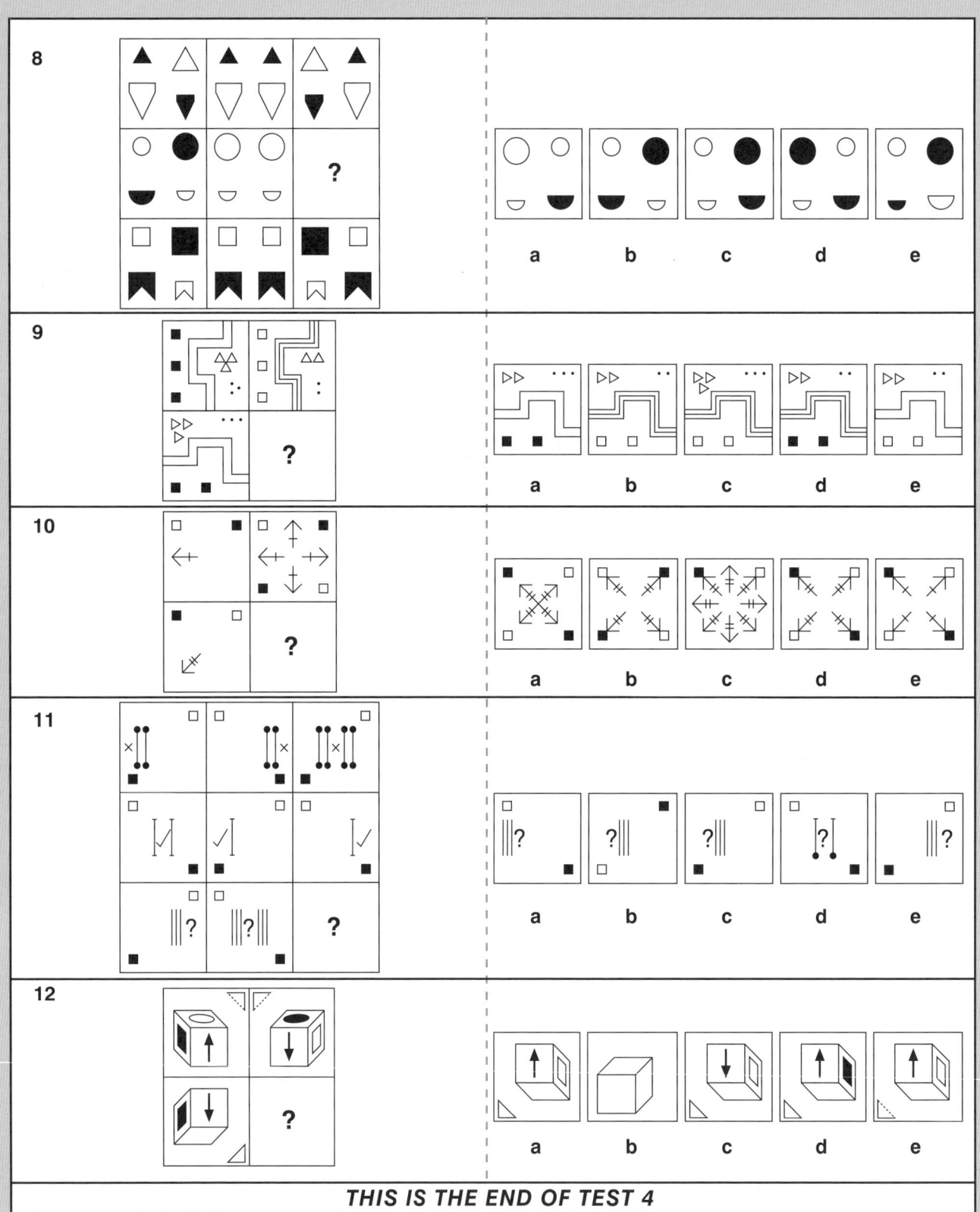

11+ Non-verbal Reasoning

Multiple-choice Test Papers
Pack 1
Answer sheets

The answer sheets for Bond 11+ Test papers Multiple-choice version are in this booklet. Please ensure you are using the correct answer sheet for the test you are taking.

OXFORD
UNIVERSITY PRESS

Great Clarendon Street, Oxford, OX2 6DP, United Kingdom

Oxford University Press is a department of the University of Oxford. It furthers the University's objective of excellence in research, scholarship, and education by publishing worldwide. Oxford is a registered trade mark of Oxford University Press in the UK and in certain other countries

Text © Andrew Baines 2015
Illustrations © Oxford University Press 2015

The moral rights of the authors have been asserted

First published in 2015

All rights reserved. No part of this publication may be reproduced, stored in a retrieval system, or transmitted, in any form or by any means, without the prior permission in writing of Oxford University Press, or as expressly permitted by law, by licence or under terms agreed with the appropriate reprographics rights organization. Enquiries concerning reproduction outside the scope of the above should be sent to the Rights Department, Oxford University Press, at the address above.

You must not circulate this work in any other form and you must impose this same condition on any acquirer

British Library Cataloguing in Publication Data
Data available

978-0-19-274087-8

Paper used in the production of this book is a natural, recyclable product made from wood grown in sustainable forests. The manufacturing process conforms to the environmental regulations of the country of origin.

Printed in China

Acknowledgements

The publishers would like to thank the following for permissions to use copyright material:

Cover illustrations: Lo Cole

Although we have made every effort to trace and contact all copyright holders before publication this has not been possible in all cases. If notified, the publisher will rectify any errors or omissions at the earliest opportunity.

Links to third party websites are provided by Oxford in good faith and for information only. Oxford disclaims any responsibility for the materials contained in any third party website referenced in this work.

The manufacturer's authorised representative in the EU for product safety is Oxford University Press España S.A. of El Parque Empresarial San Fernando de Henares, Avenida de Castilla, 2 – 28830 Madrid (www.oup.es/en or product.safety@oup.com). OUP España S.A. also acts as importer into Spain of products made by the manufacturer.

Bond 11+ Non-verbal Reasoning Test 1

Name

Bond 11+ Non-verbal Reasoning Test 2

Name

OXFORD
UNIVERSITY PRESS

Bond 11+ Non-verbal Reasoning Test 3

Name

Section 1

Example	Practice 1	Practice 2	1	2	3	4	5	6	7	8	9	10	11	12
a	a	a	a	a	a	a	a	a	a	a	a	a	a	a
b	b	b	b	b	b	b	b	b	b	b	b	b	b	b
c	c	c	c	c	c	c	c	c	c	c	c	c	c	c
d	d	d	d	d	d	d	d	d	d	d	d	d	d	d
e	e	e	e	e	e	e	e	e	e	e	e	e	e	e

Section 2

Example	Practice 1	Practice 2	1	2	3	4	5	6	7	8	9	10	11	12
a	a	a	a	a	a	a	a	a	a	a	a	a	a	a
b	b	b	b	b	b	b	b	b	b	b	b	b	b	b
c	c	c	c	c	c	c	c	c	c	c	c	c	c	c
d	d	d	d	d	d	d	d	d	d	d	d	d	d	d
e	e	e	e	e	e	e	e	e	e	e	e	e	e	e

Section 3

Example	Practice 1	Practice 2	1	2	3	4	5	6	7	8	9	10	11	12
a	a	a	a	a	a	a	a	a	a	a	a	a	a	a
b	b	b	b	b	b	b	b	b	b	b	b	b	b	b
c	c	c	c	c	c	c	c	c	c	c	c	c	c	c
d	d	d	d	d	d	d	d	d	d	d	d	d	d	d
e	e	e	e	e	e	e	e	e	e	e	e	e	e	e

Section 4

Example	Practice 1	Practice 2	1	2	3	4	5	6	7	8	9	10	11	12
a	a	a	a	a	a	a	a	a	a	a	a	a	a	a
b	b	b	b	b	b	b	b	b	b	b	b	b	b	b
c	c	c	c	c	c	c	c	c	c	c	c	c	c	c
d	d	d	d	d	d	d	d	d	d	d	d	d	d	d
e	e	e	e	e	e	e	e	e	e	e	e	e	e	e

Section 5

Example	Practice 1	Practice 2	1	2	3	4	5	6	7	8	9	10	11	12
a	a	a	a	a	a	a	a	a	a	a	a	a	a	a
b	b	b	b	b	b	b	b	b	b	b	b	b	b	b
c	c	c	c	c	c	c	c	c	c	c	c	c	c	c
d	d	d	d	d	d	d	d	d	d	d	d	d	d	d
e	e	e	e	e	e	e	e	e	e	e	e	e	e	e

Notes

Notes

Notes

11+
Non-verbal Reasoning

Multiple-choice Test Papers
Pack 1
Test 1

Read the following:

- Do not begin the test or open this booklet until told to do so. Follow the instructions for sitting the test
- Work as quickly and as carefully as you can
- Answers should be marked in the answer booklet provided, not in this test booklet
- You may do rough working on a separate sheet of paper
- Be careful to keep your place in the accompanying answer booklet
- You will have 30 minutes to complete the test

OXFORD
UNIVERSITY PRESS

Great Clarendon Street, Oxford, OX2 6DP, United Kingdom

Oxford University Press is a department of the University of Oxford. It furthers the University's objective of excellence in research, scholarship, and education by publishing worldwide. Oxford is a registered trade mark of Oxford University Press in the UK and in certain other countries

Text © Andrew Baines 2015
Illustrations © Oxford University Press 2015

The moral rights of the authors have been asserted

First published in 2015

All rights reserved. No part of this publication may be reproduced, stored in a retrieval system, or transmitted, in any form or by any means, without the prior permission in writing of Oxford University Press, or as expressly permitted by law, by licence or under terms agreed with the appropriate reprographics rights organization. Enquiries concerning reproduction outside the scope of the above should be sent to the Rights Department, Oxford University Press, at the address above.

You must not circulate this work in any other form and you must impose this same condition on any acquirer

British Library Cataloguing in Publication Data
Data available

978-0-19-274087-8

Paper used in the production of this book is a natural, recyclable product made from wood grown in sustainable forests. The manufacturing process conforms to the environmental regulations of the country of origin.

Printed in China

Acknowledgements

The publishers would like to thank the following for permissions to use copyright material:

Cover illustrations: Lo Cole

Although we have made every effort to trace and contact all copyright holders before publication this has not been possible in all cases. If notified, the publisher will rectify any errors or omissions at the earliest opportunity.

Links to third party websites are provided by Oxford in good faith and for information only. Oxford disclaims any responsibility for the materials contained in any third party website referenced in this work.

The manufacturer's authorised representative in the EU for product safety is Oxford University Press España S.A. of El Parque Empresarial San Fernando de Henares, Avenida de Castilla, 2 – 28830 Madrid (www.oup.es/en or product.safety@oup.com). OUP España S.A. also acts as importer into Spain of products made by the manufacturer.

Section 1

Which shape or pattern on the right completes the second pair in the same way as the first pair?

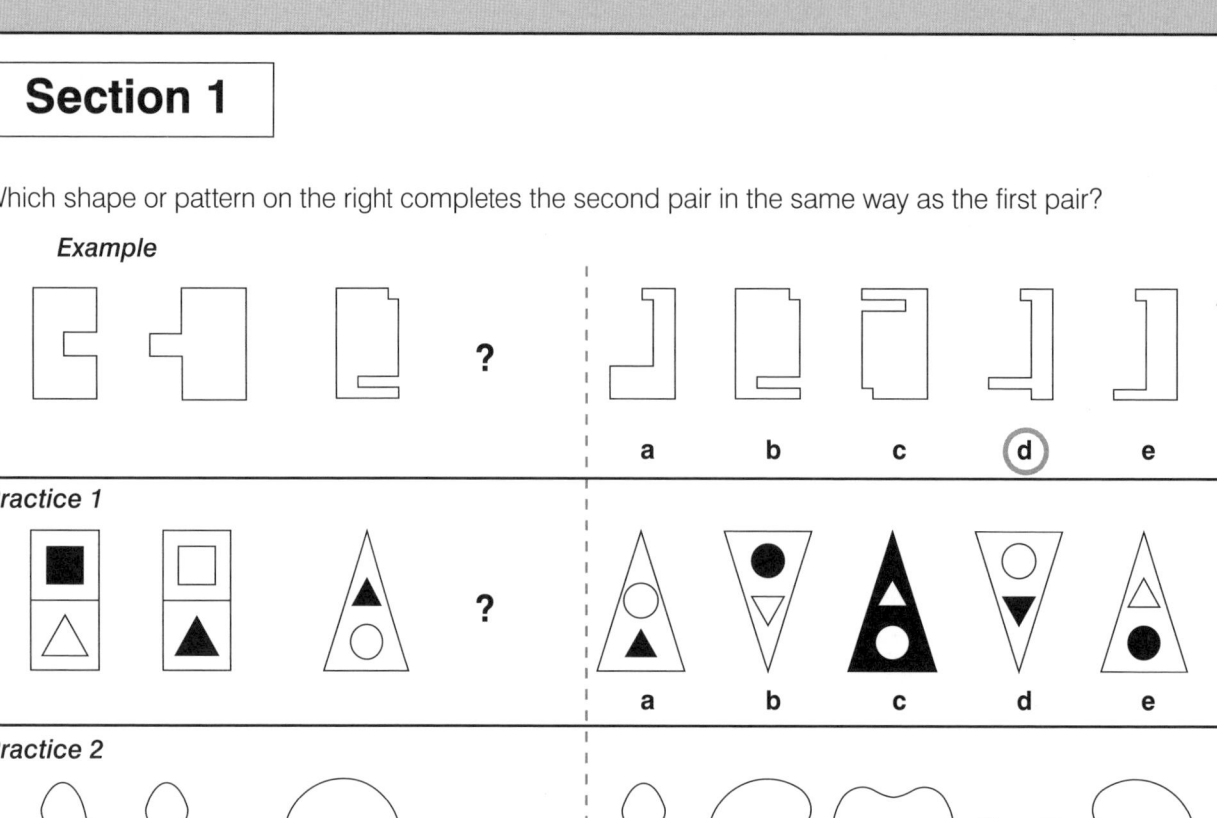

YOU NOW HAVE SIX MINUTES TO COMPLETE THE REST OF SECTION 1

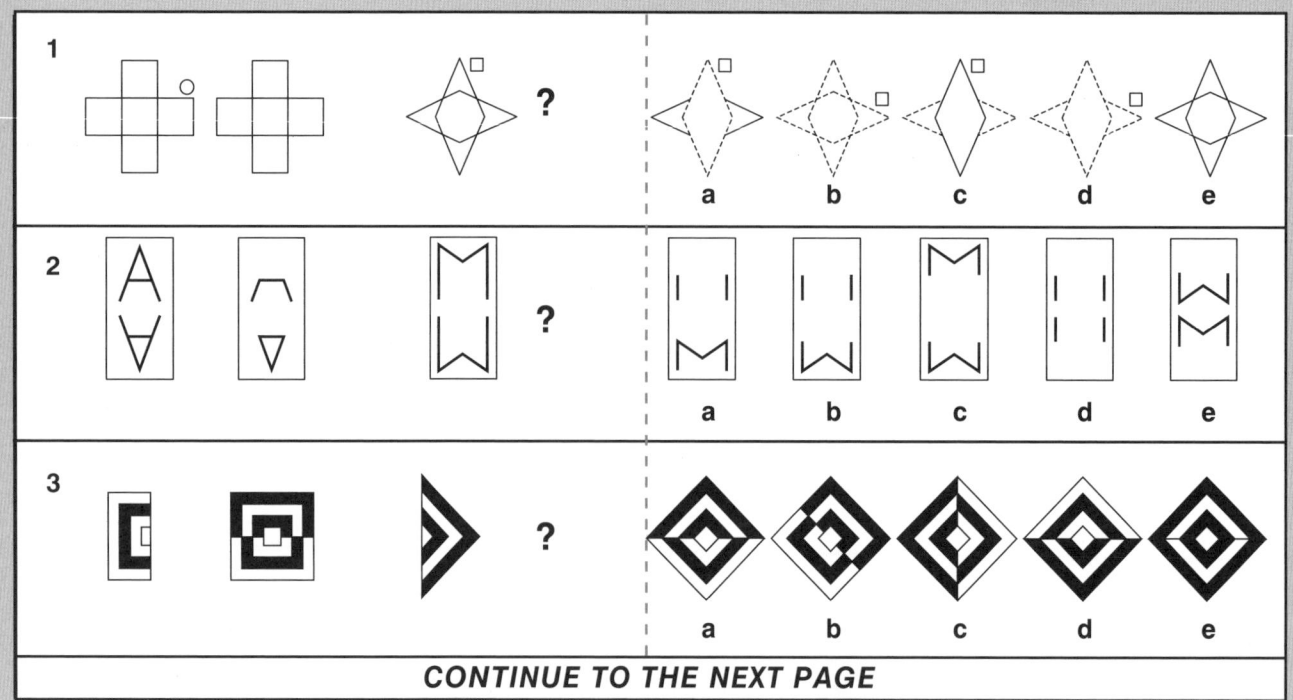

CONTINUE TO THE NEXT PAGE

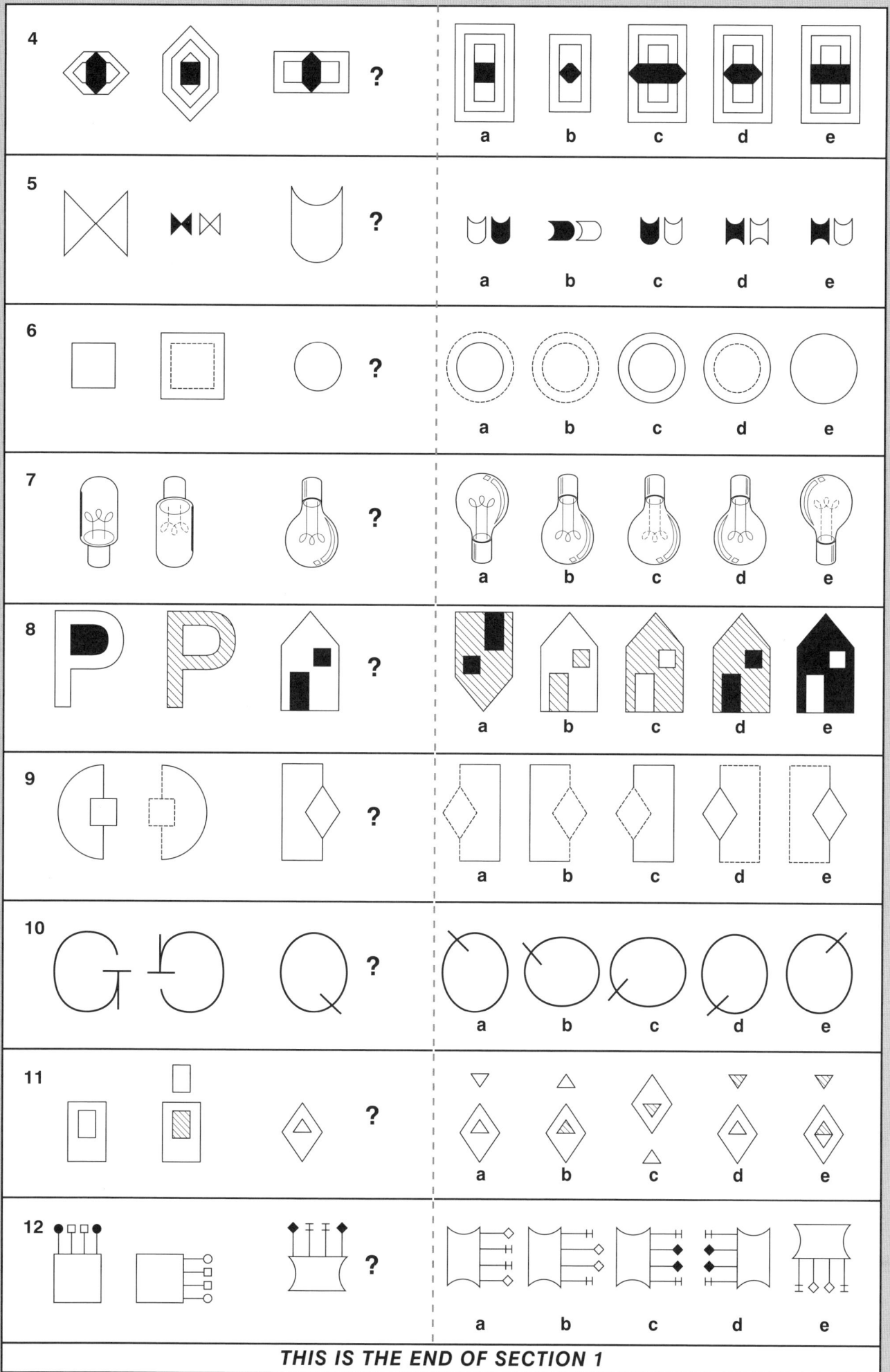

Section 2

Which shape or pattern on the right belongs to the group on the left?

Example

a b c d (e)

Practice 1

a b c d e

Practice 2

a b c d e

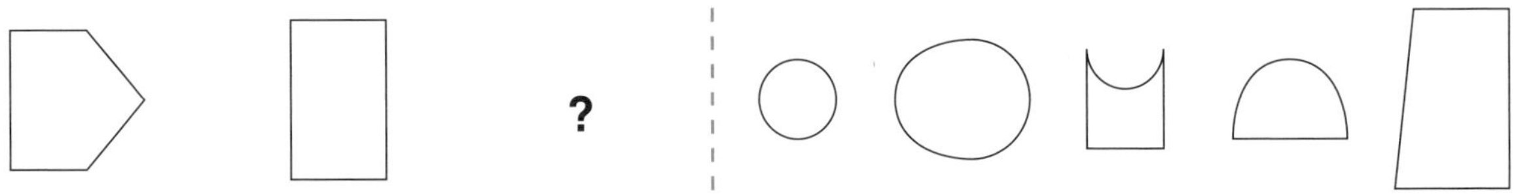

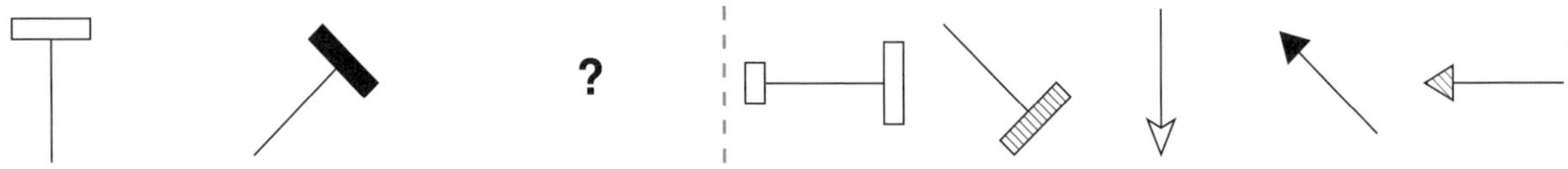

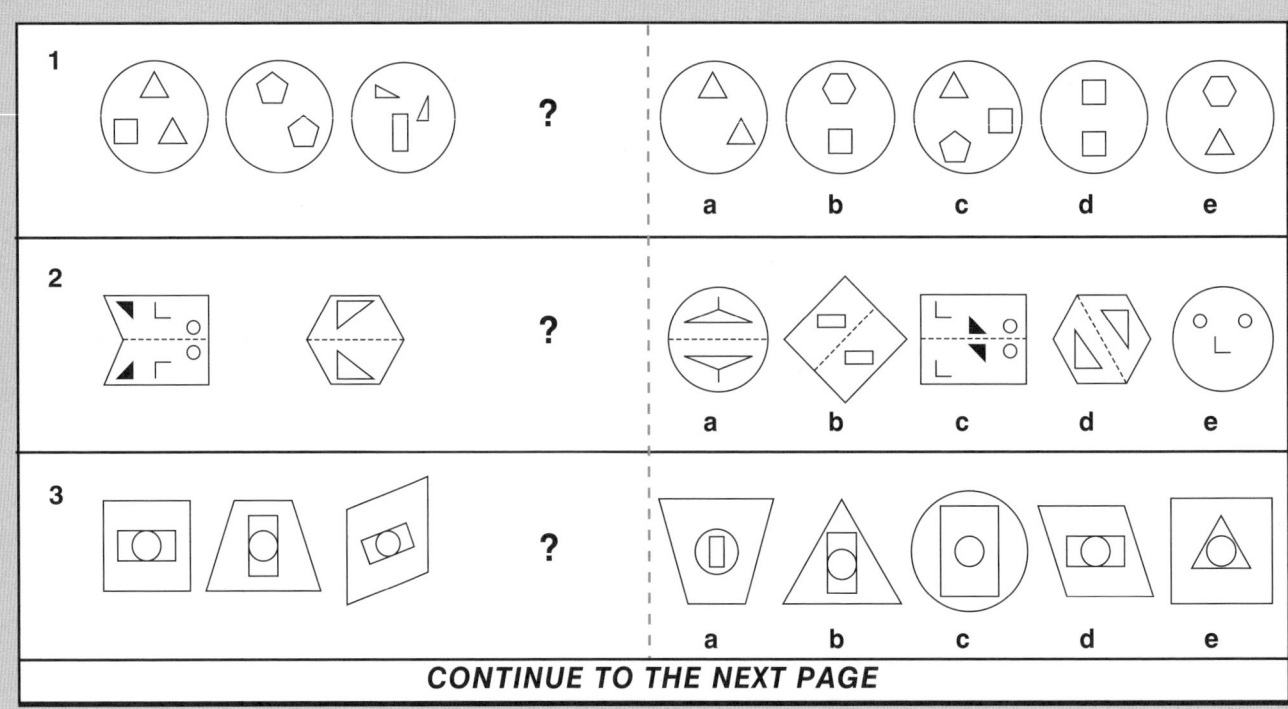

YOU NOW HAVE SIX MINUTES TO COMPLETE THE REST OF SECTION 2

1

a b c d e

2

a b c d e

3

a b c d e

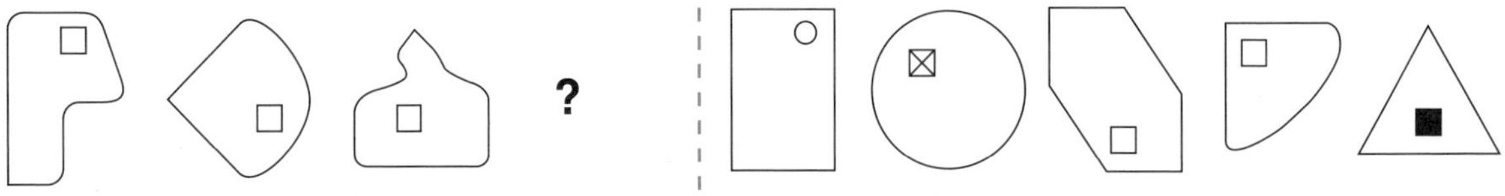

CONTINUE TO THE NEXT PAGE

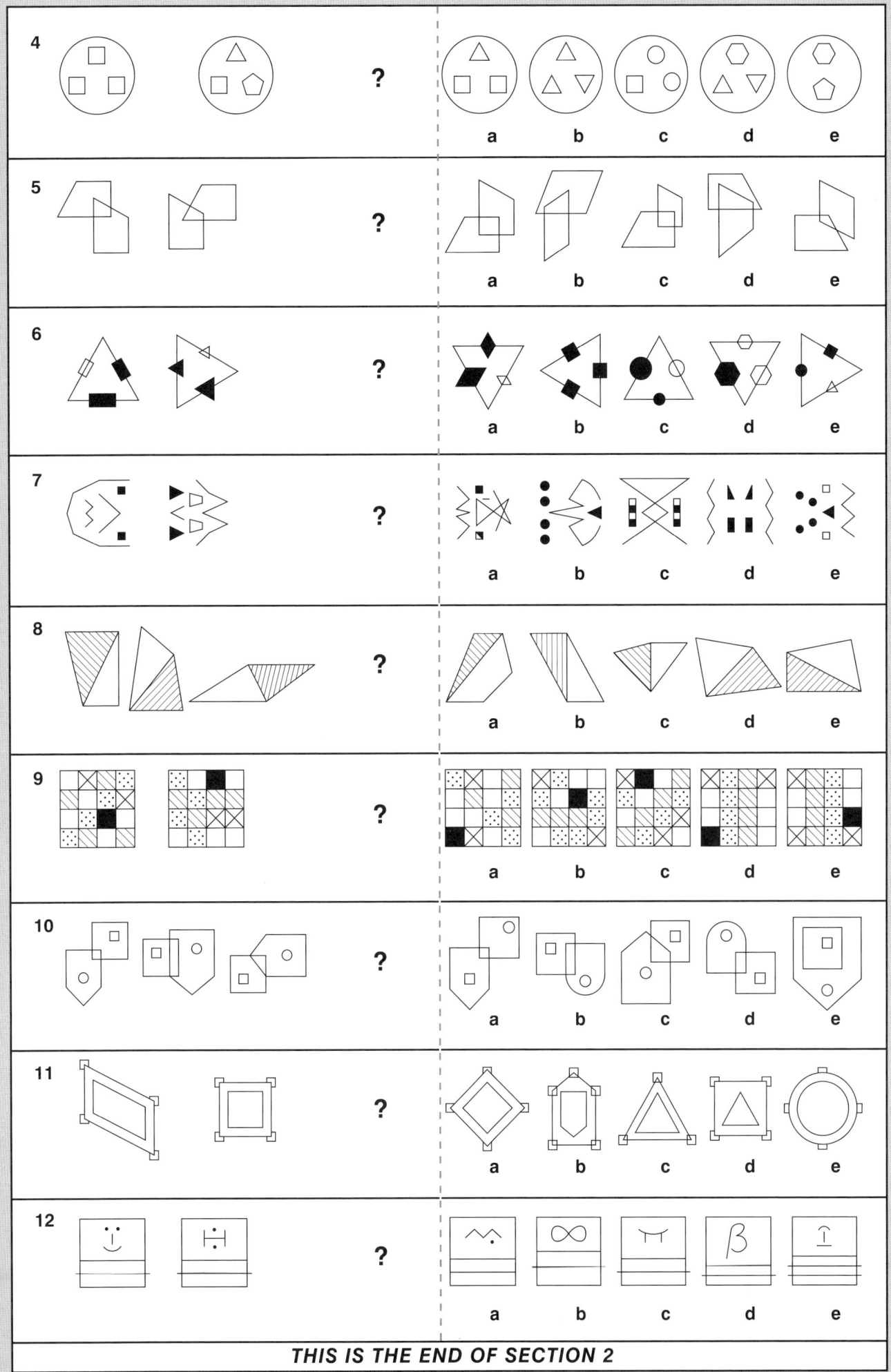

Section 3

Which one comes next?

Example

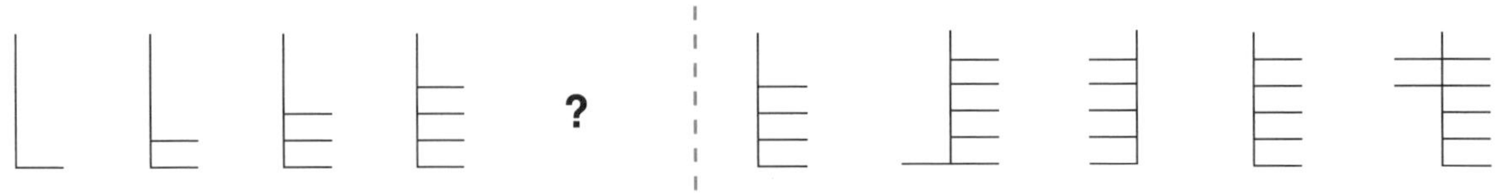

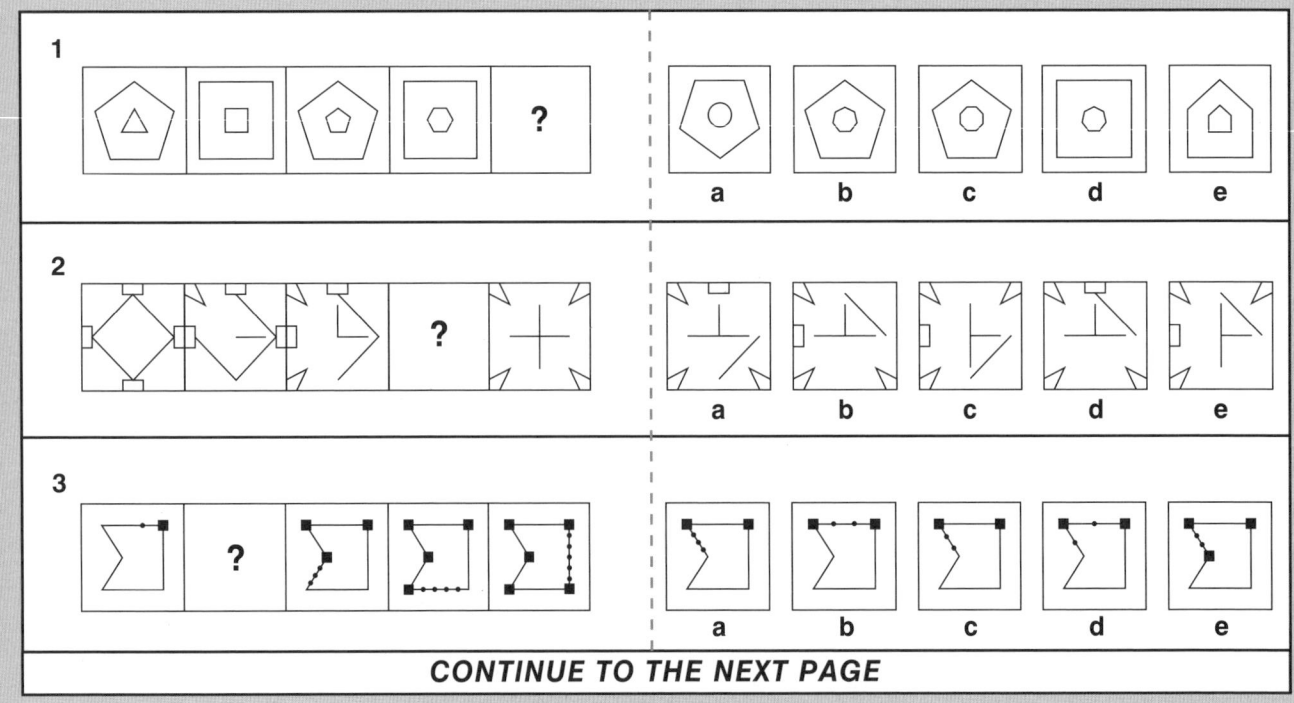

a b c (d) e

Practice 1

a b c d e

Practice 2

a b c d e

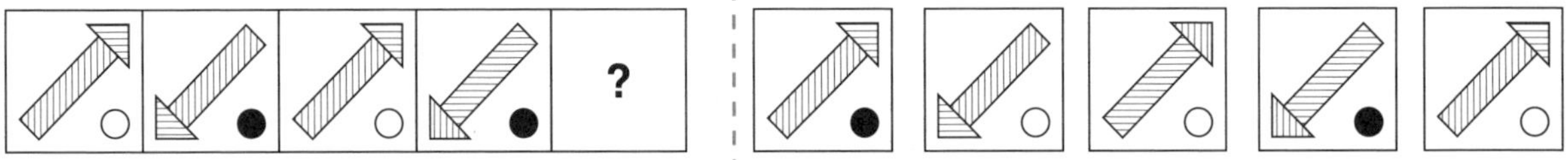

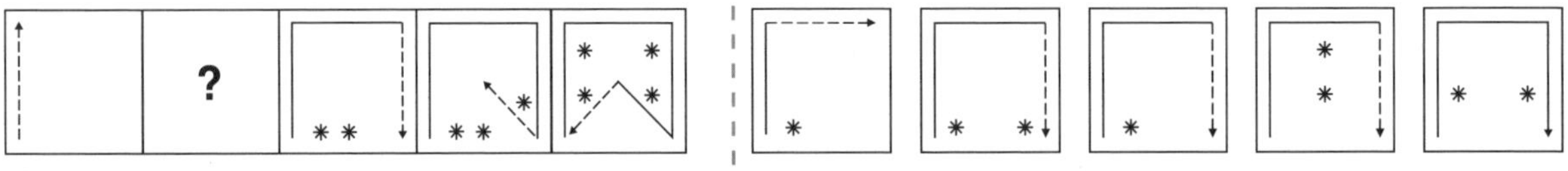

YOU NOW HAVE SIX MINUTES TO COMPLETE THE REST OF SECTION 3

1

a b c d e

2

a b c d e

3

a b c d e

CONTINUE TO THE NEXT PAGE

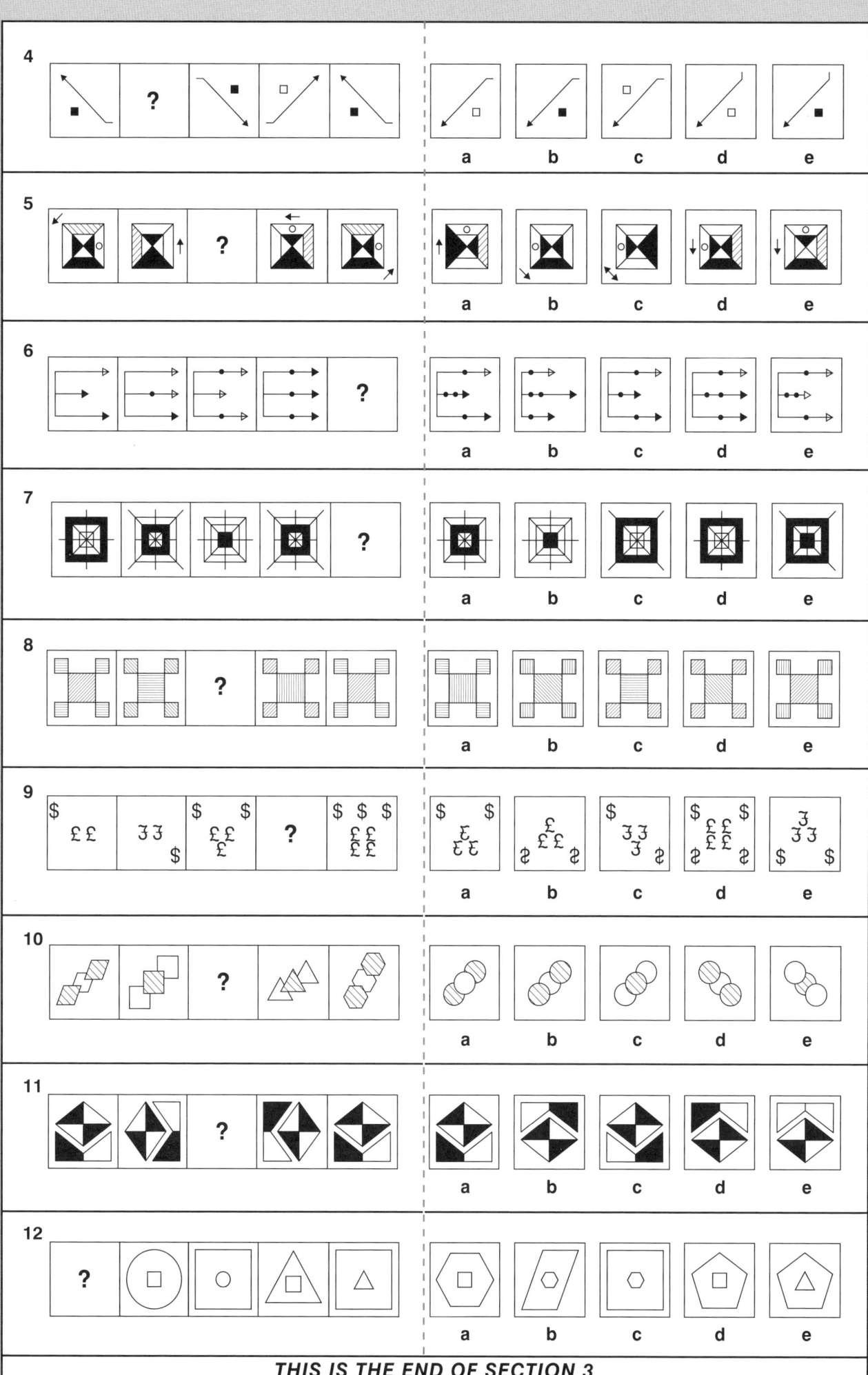

Section 4

Which code matches the shape or pattern given at the end of each line?

Example

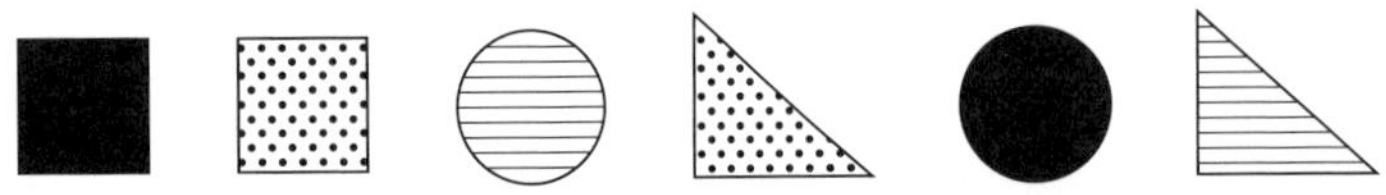

							BZ	AZ	CX	BY	CZ
AX	AY	BZ	CY	BX	?		a	b	c	d	(e)

Practice 1

					RY	SX	RS	SY	RX
RX	SX	RY	?		a	b	c	d	e

Practice 2

					QE	PF	QF	PE	PG
PE	PF	QG	?		a	b	c	d	e

YOU NOW HAVE SIX MINUTES TO COMPLETE THE REST OF SECTION 4

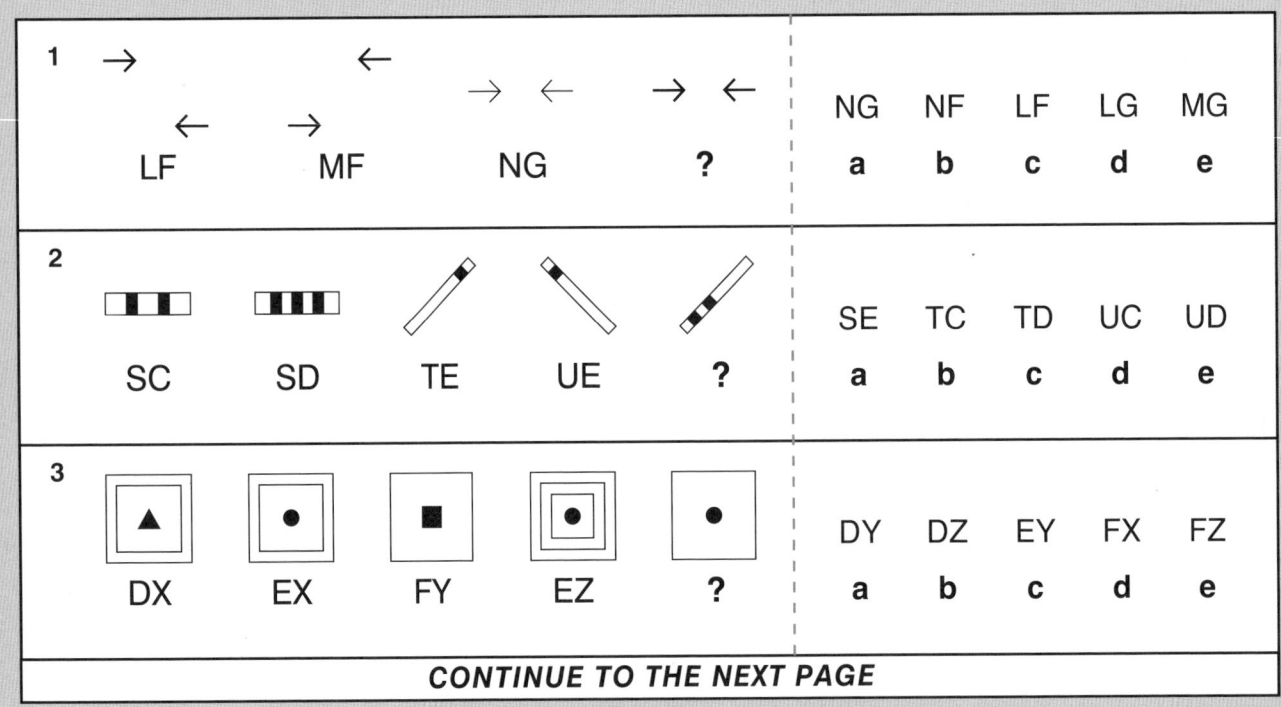

CONTINUE TO THE NEXT PAGE

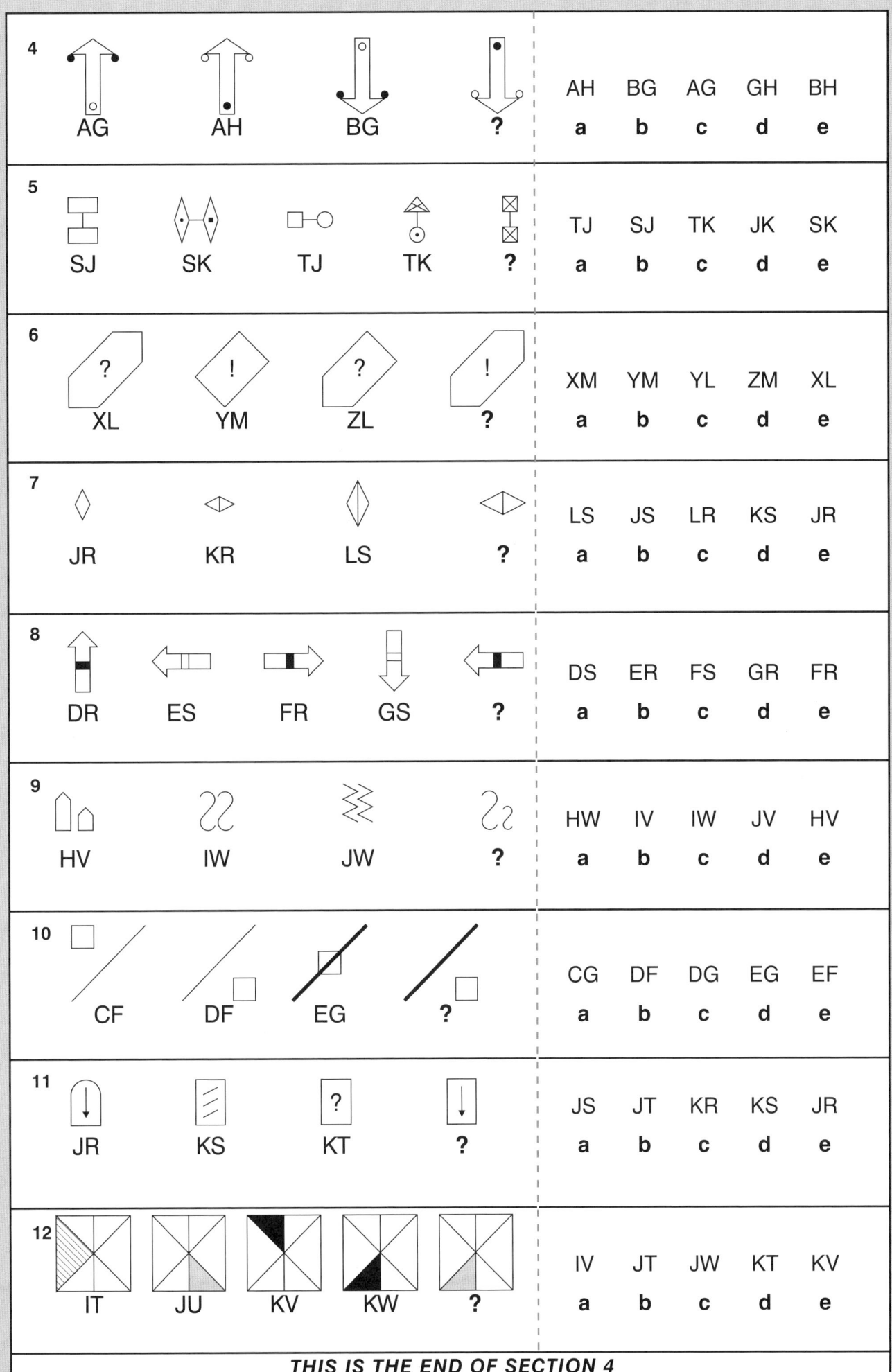

Section 5

Which shape or pattern completes the larger square?

Example

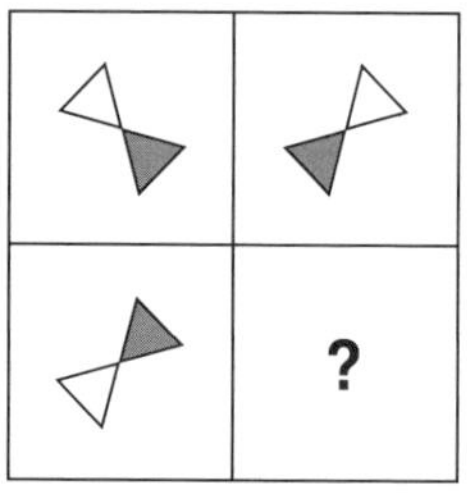

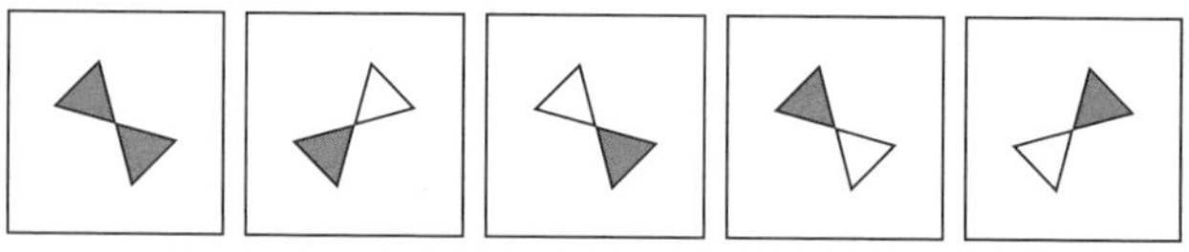

a b c (d) e

Practice 1

a b c d e

Practice 2

a b c d e

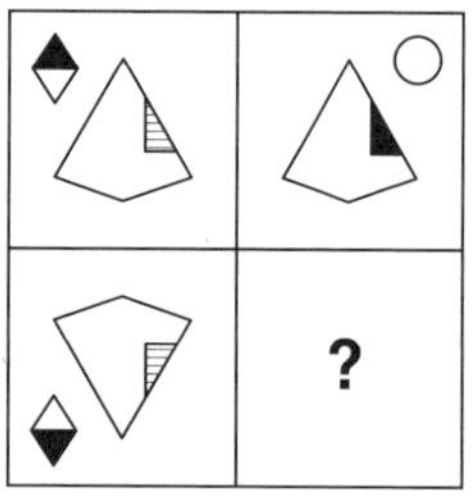

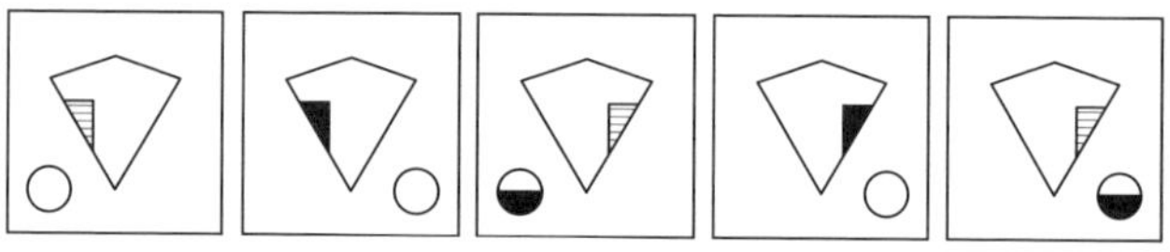

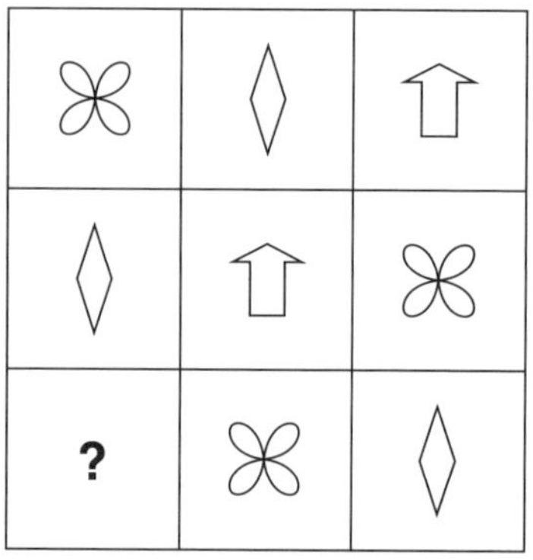

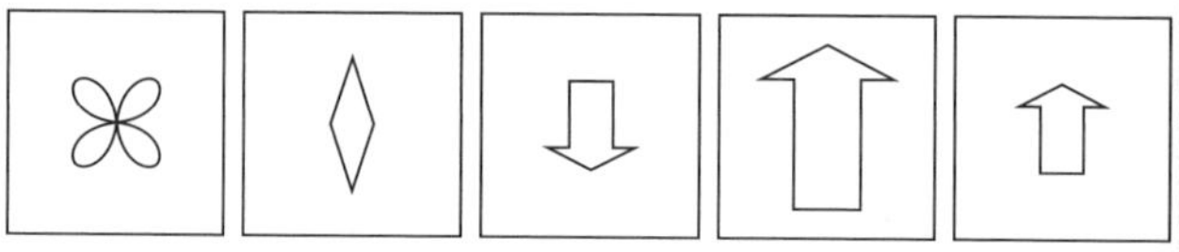

YOU NOW HAVE SIX MINUTES TO COMPLETE THE REST OF SECTION 5

1

a b c d e

2

a b c d e

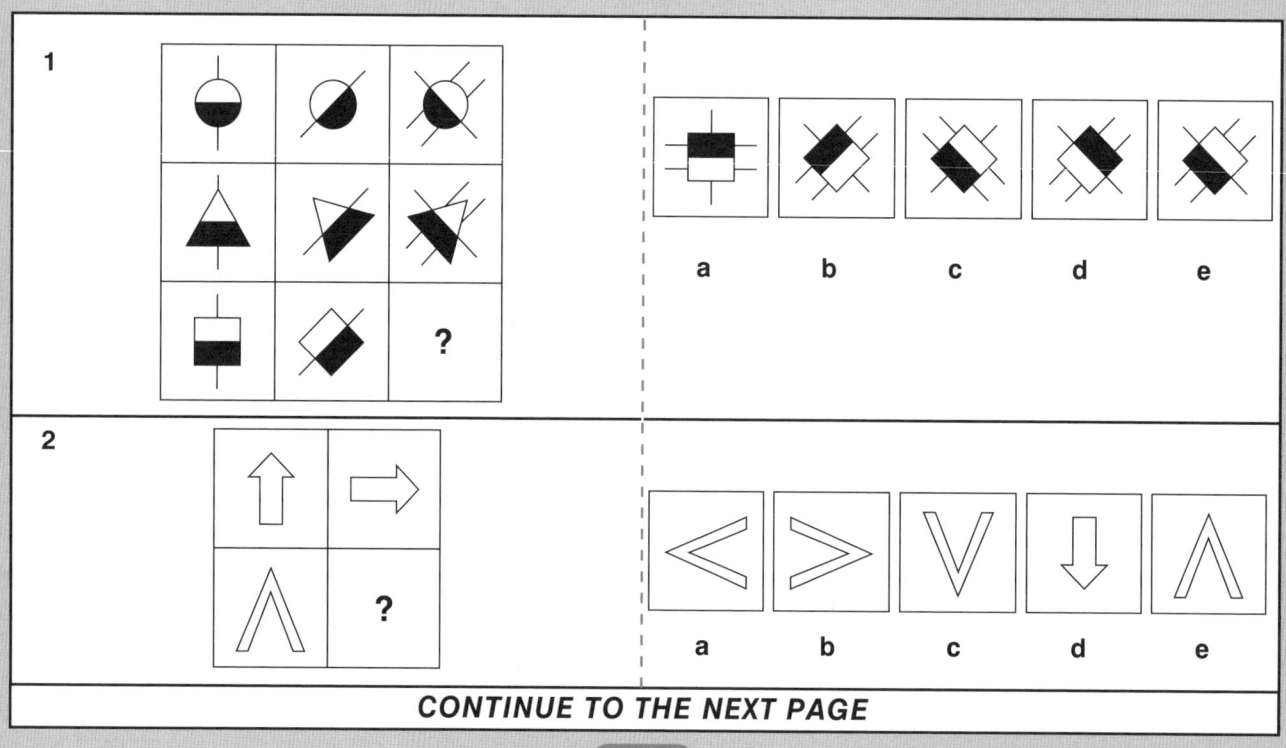

CONTINUE TO THE NEXT PAGE

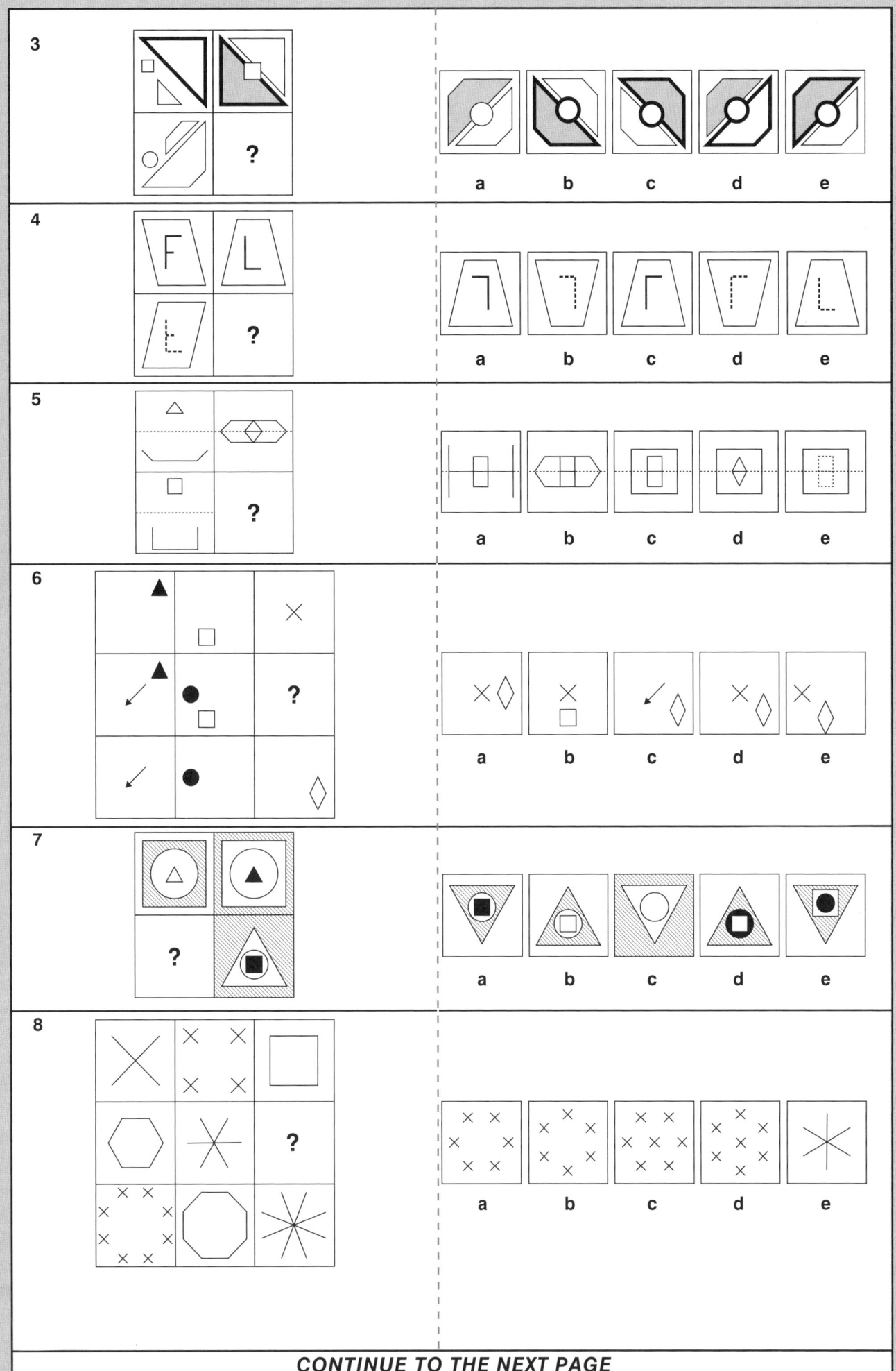

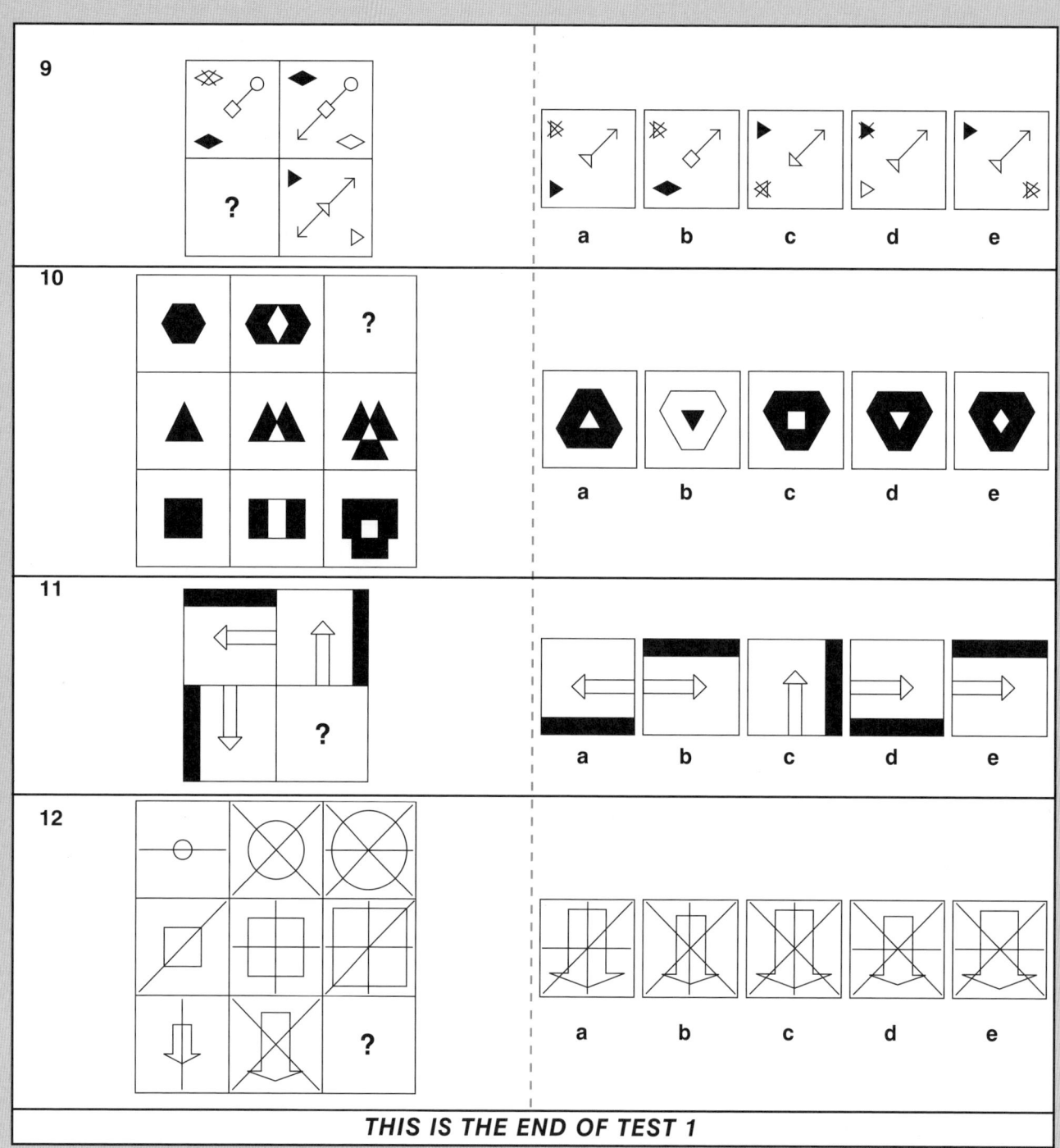

THIS IS THE END OF TEST 1

11+ Non-verbal Reasoning

Multiple-choice Test Papers
Pack 1
Test 2

Read the following:

- Do not begin the test or open this booklet until told to do so. Follow the instructions for sitting the test
- Work as quickly and as carefully as you can
- Answers should be marked in the answer booklet provided, not in this test booklet
- You may do rough working on a separate sheet of paper
- Be careful to keep your place in the accompanying answer booklet
- You will have 30 minutes to complete the test

OXFORD
UNIVERSITY PRESS

Great Clarendon Street, Oxford, OX2 6DP, United Kingdom

Oxford University Press is a department of the University of Oxford. It furthers the University's objective of excellence in research, scholarship, and education by publishing worldwide. Oxford is a registered trade mark of Oxford University Press in the UK and in certain other countries

Text © Andrew Baines 2015
Illustrations © Oxford University Press 2015

The moral rights of the authors have been asserted

First published in 2015

All rights reserved. No part of this publication may be reproduced, stored in a retrieval system, or transmitted, in any form or by any means, without the prior permission in writing of Oxford University Press, or as expressly permitted by law, by licence or under terms agreed with the appropriate reprographics rights organization. Enquiries concerning reproduction outside the scope of the above should be sent to the Rights Department, Oxford University Press, at the address above.

You must not circulate this work in any other form and you must impose this same condition on any acquirer

British Library Cataloguing in Publication Data
Data available

978-0-19-274087-8

Paper used in the production of this book is a natural, recyclable product made from wood grown in sustainable forests. The manufacturing process conforms to the environmental regulations of the country of origin.

Printed in China

Acknowledgements

The publishers would like to thank the following for permissions to use copyright material:

Cover illustrations: Lo Cole

Although we have made every effort to trace and contact all copyright holders before publication this has not been possible in all cases. If notified, the publisher will rectify any errors or omissions at the earliest opportunity.

Links to third party websites are provided by Oxford in good faith and for information only. Oxford disclaims any responsibility for the materials contained in any third party website referenced in this work.

The manufacturer's authorised representative in the EU for product safety is Oxford University Press España S.A. of El Parque Empresarial San Fernando de Henares, Avenida de Castilla, 2 – 28830 Madrid (www.oup.es/en or product.safety@oup.com). OUP España S.A. also acts as importer into Spain of products made by the manufacturer.

Section 1

Which shape or pattern on the right completes the second pair in the same way as the first pair?

Example

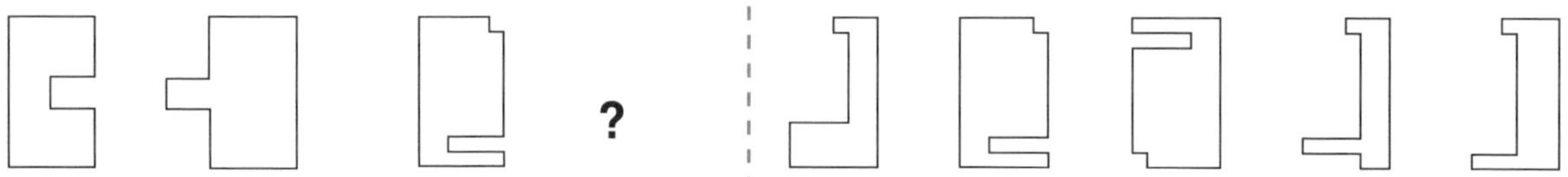

Practice 1

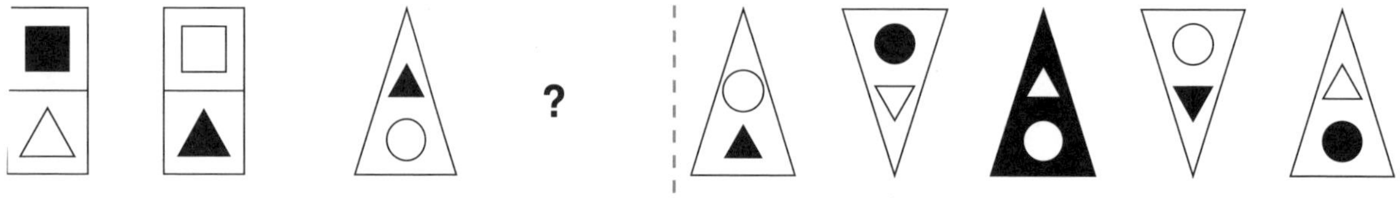

Practice 2

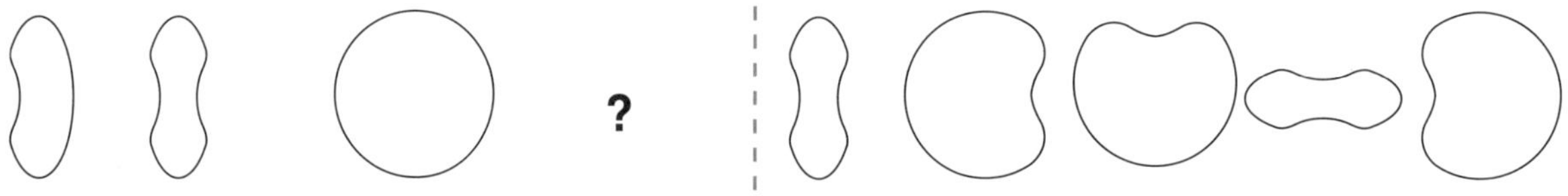

YOU NOW HAVE SIX MINUTES TO COMPLETE THE REST OF SECTION 1

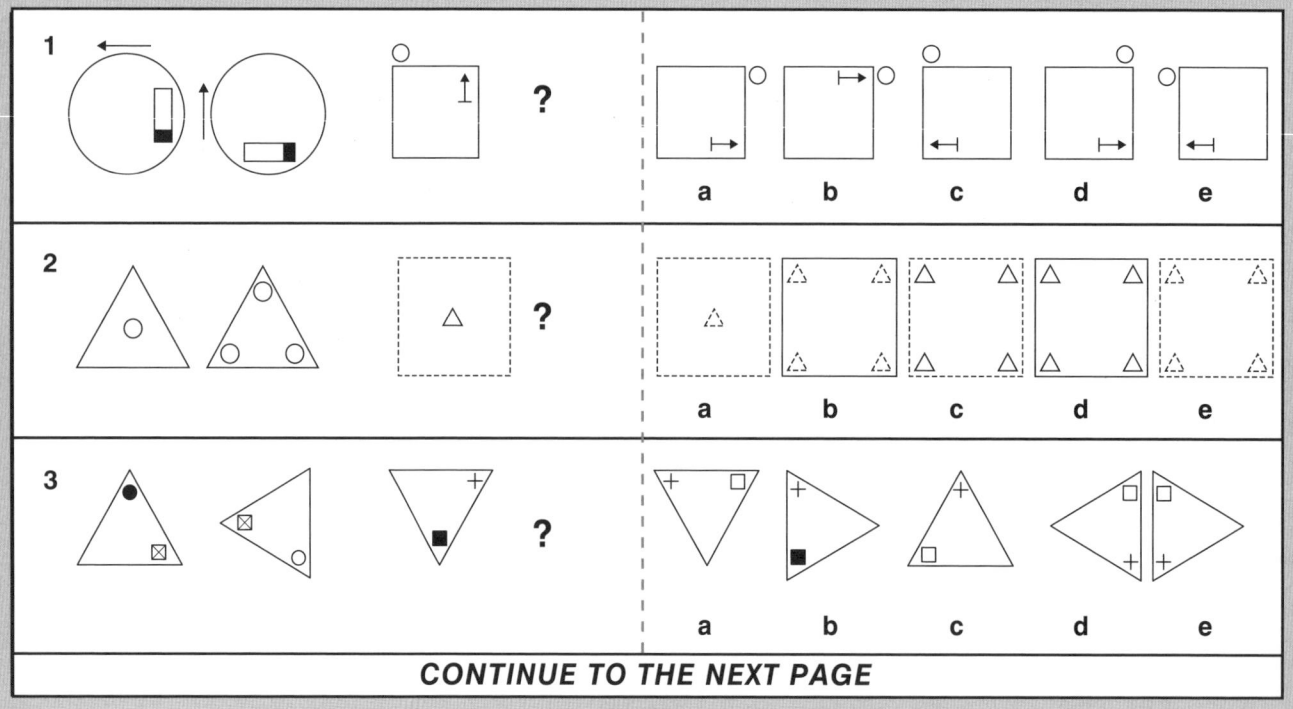

CONTINUE TO THE NEXT PAGE

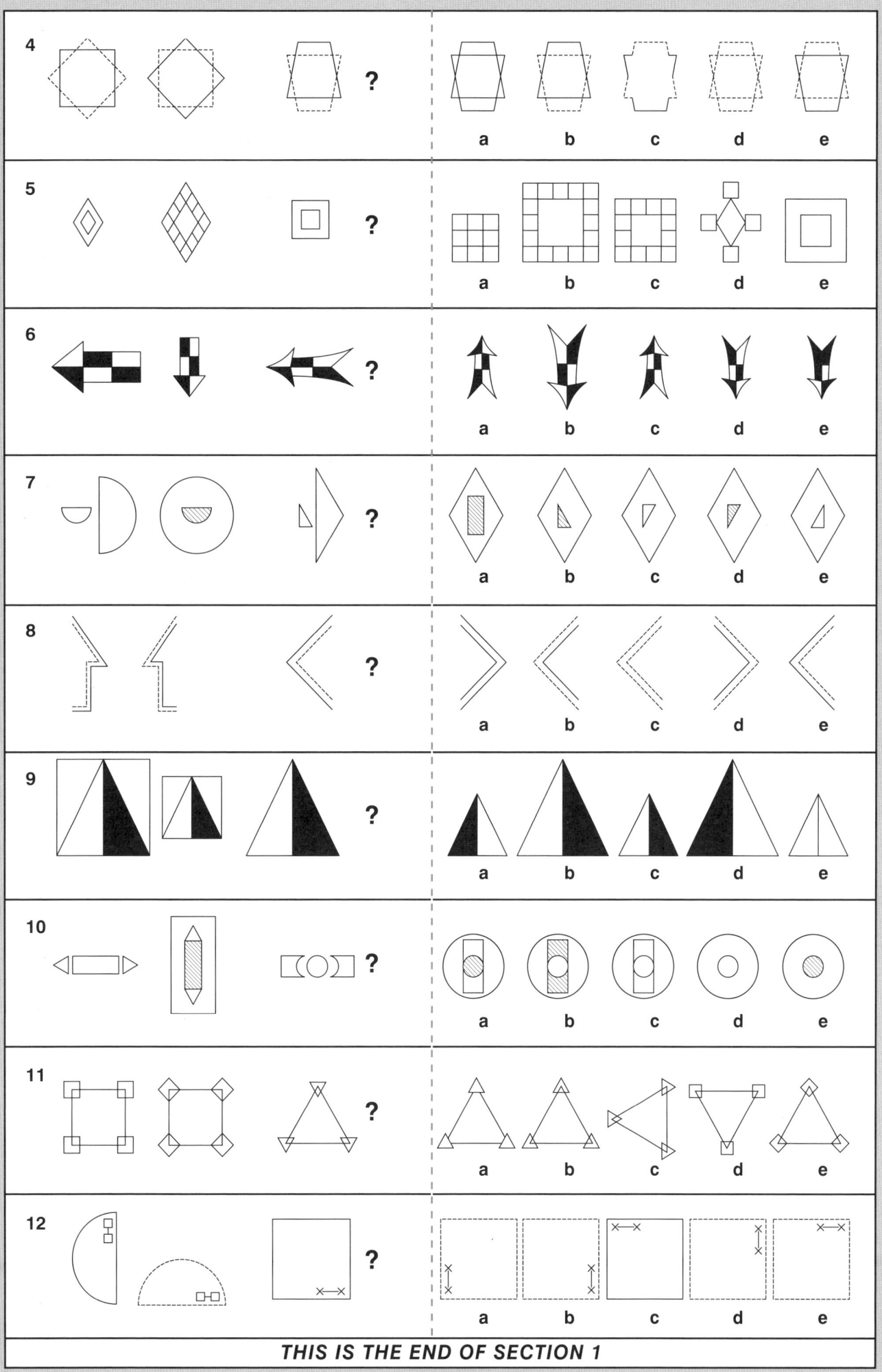

Section 2

Which shape or pattern on the right belongs to the group on the left?

Example

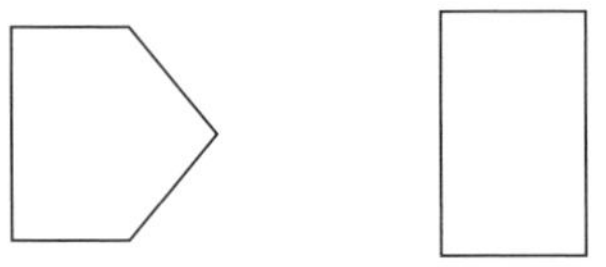

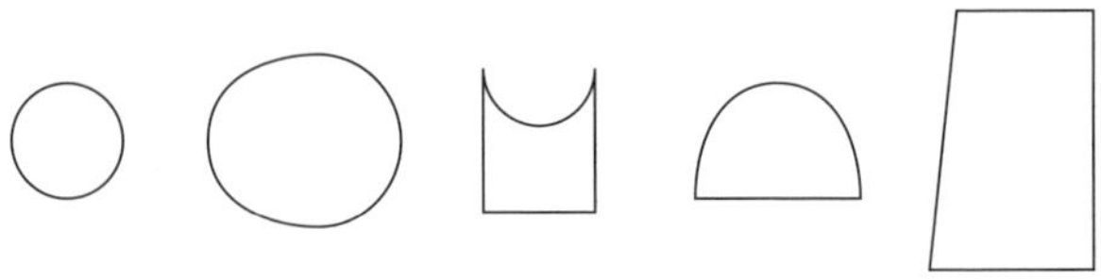

a b c d **e**

Practice 1

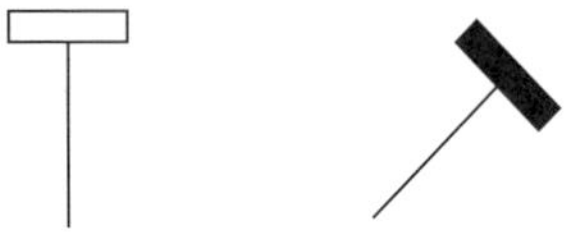

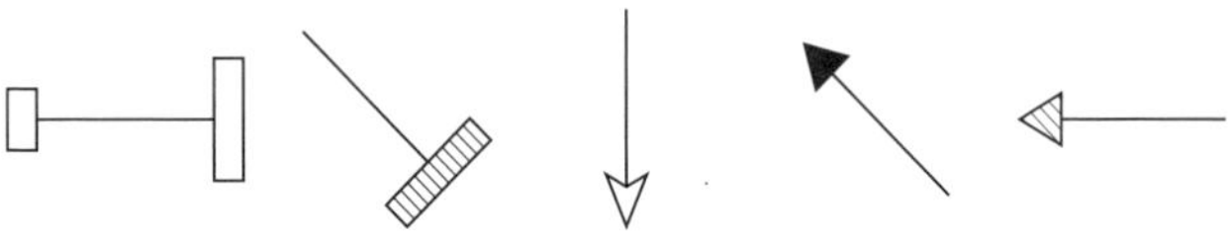

a b c d e

Practice 2

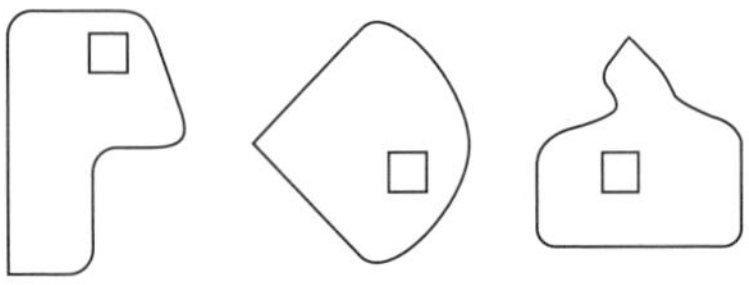

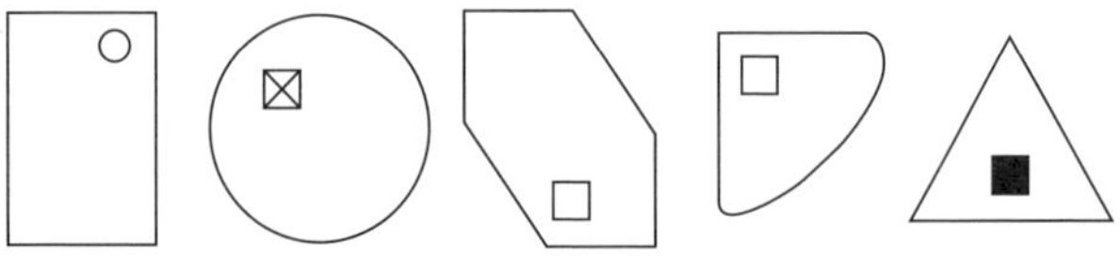

a b c d e

YOU NOW HAVE SIX MINUTES TO COMPLETE THE REST OF SECTION 2

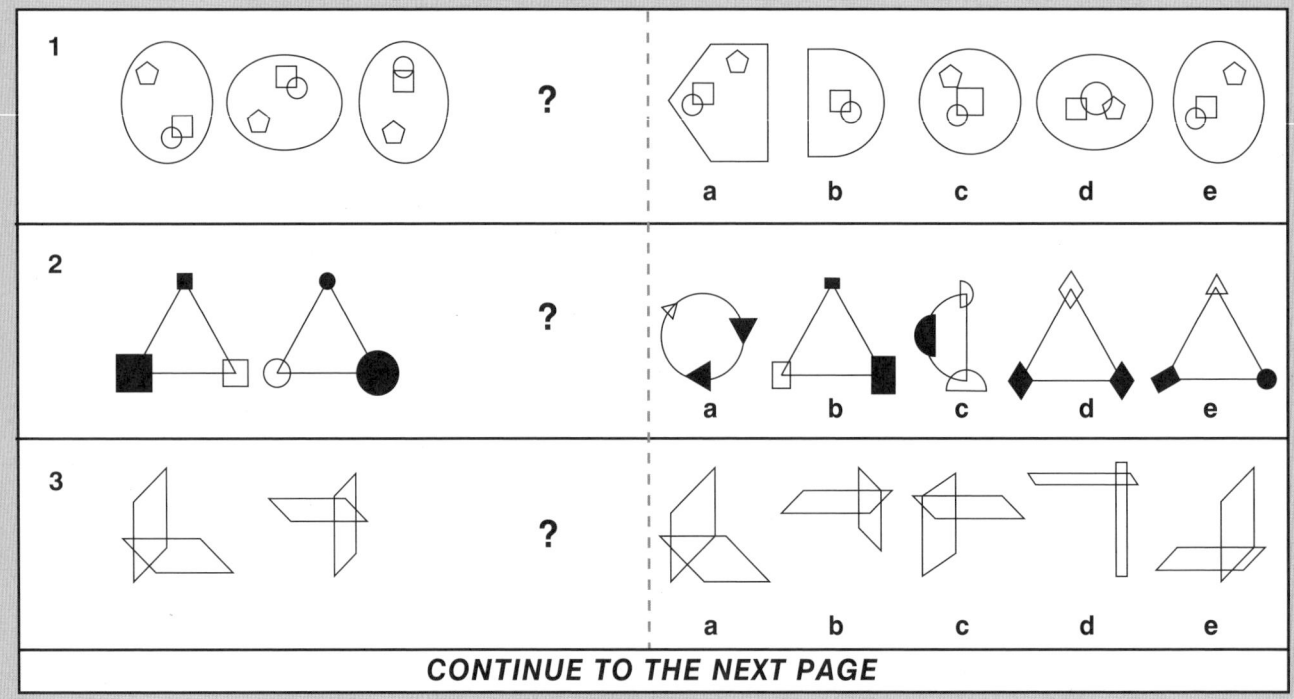

CONTINUE TO THE NEXT PAGE

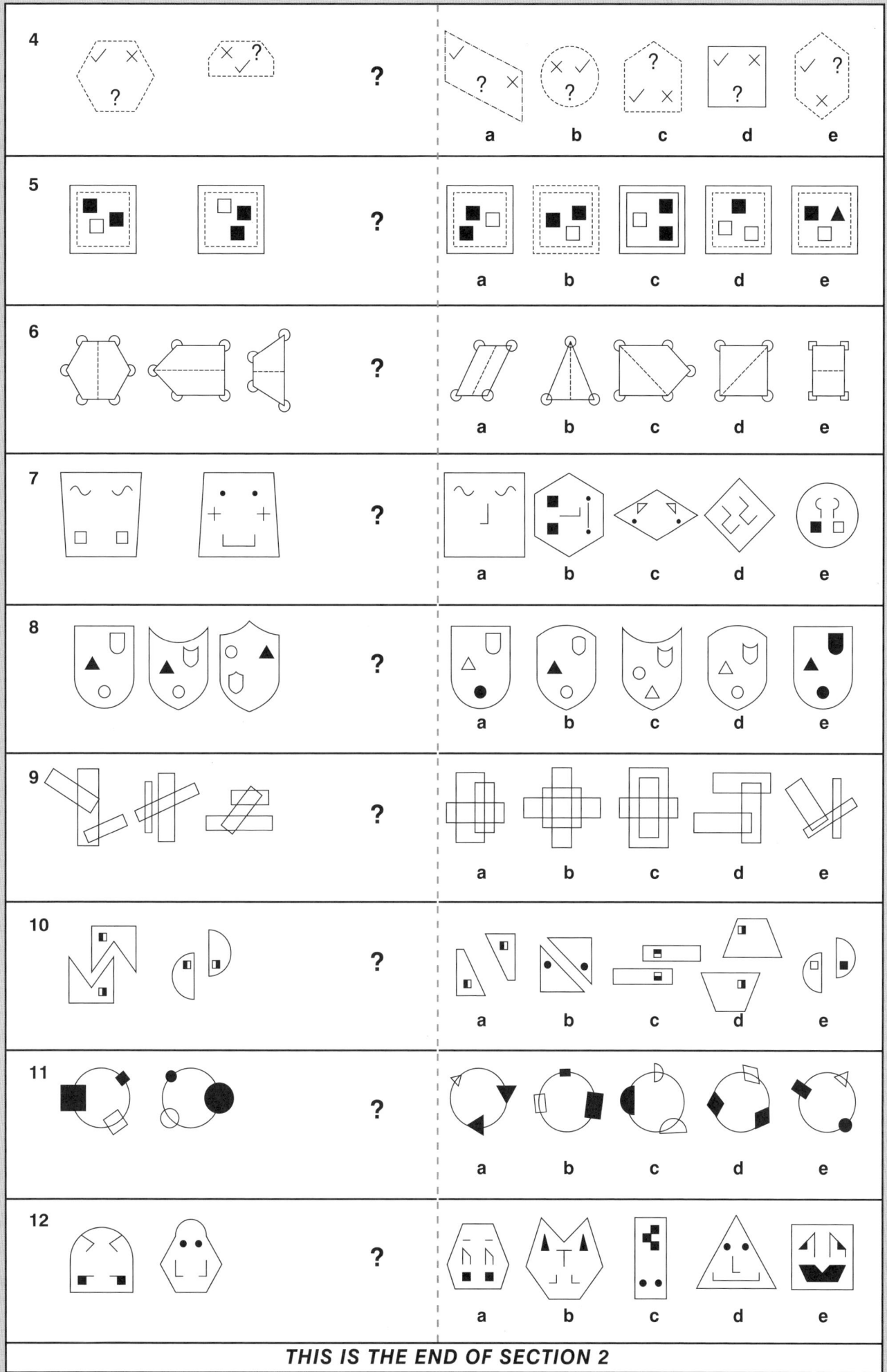

Section 3

Which one comes next?

Example

a b c d e

Practice 1

a b c d e

Practice 2

a b c d e

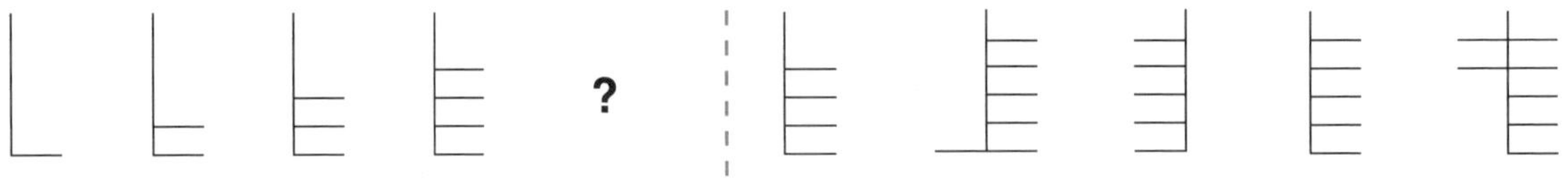

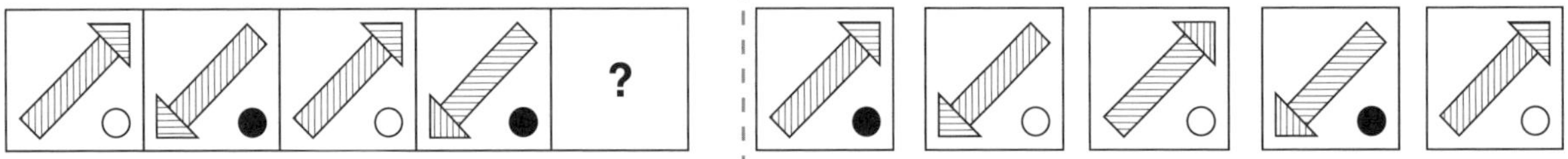

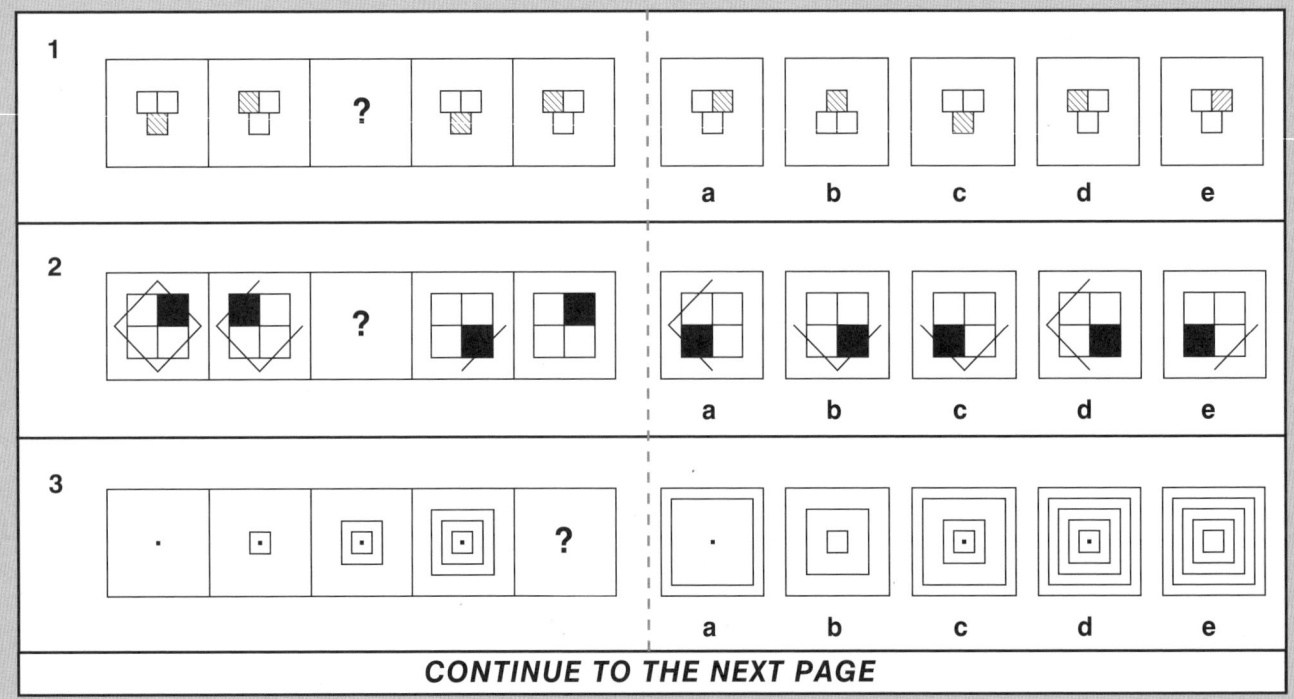

YOU NOW HAVE SIX MINUTES TO COMPLETE THE REST OF SECTION 3

1

a b c d e

2

a b c d e

3

a b c d e

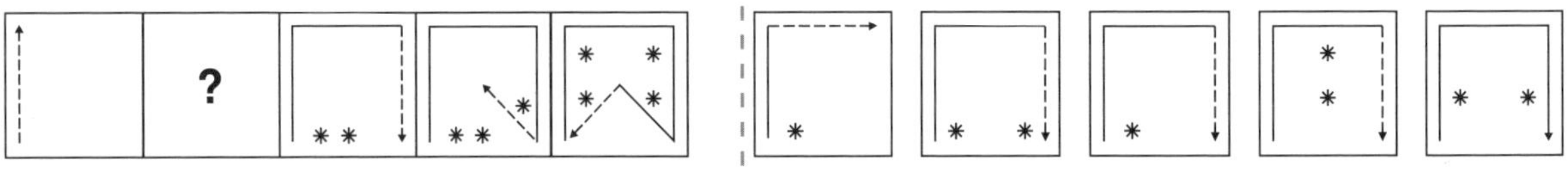

CONTINUE TO THE NEXT PAGE

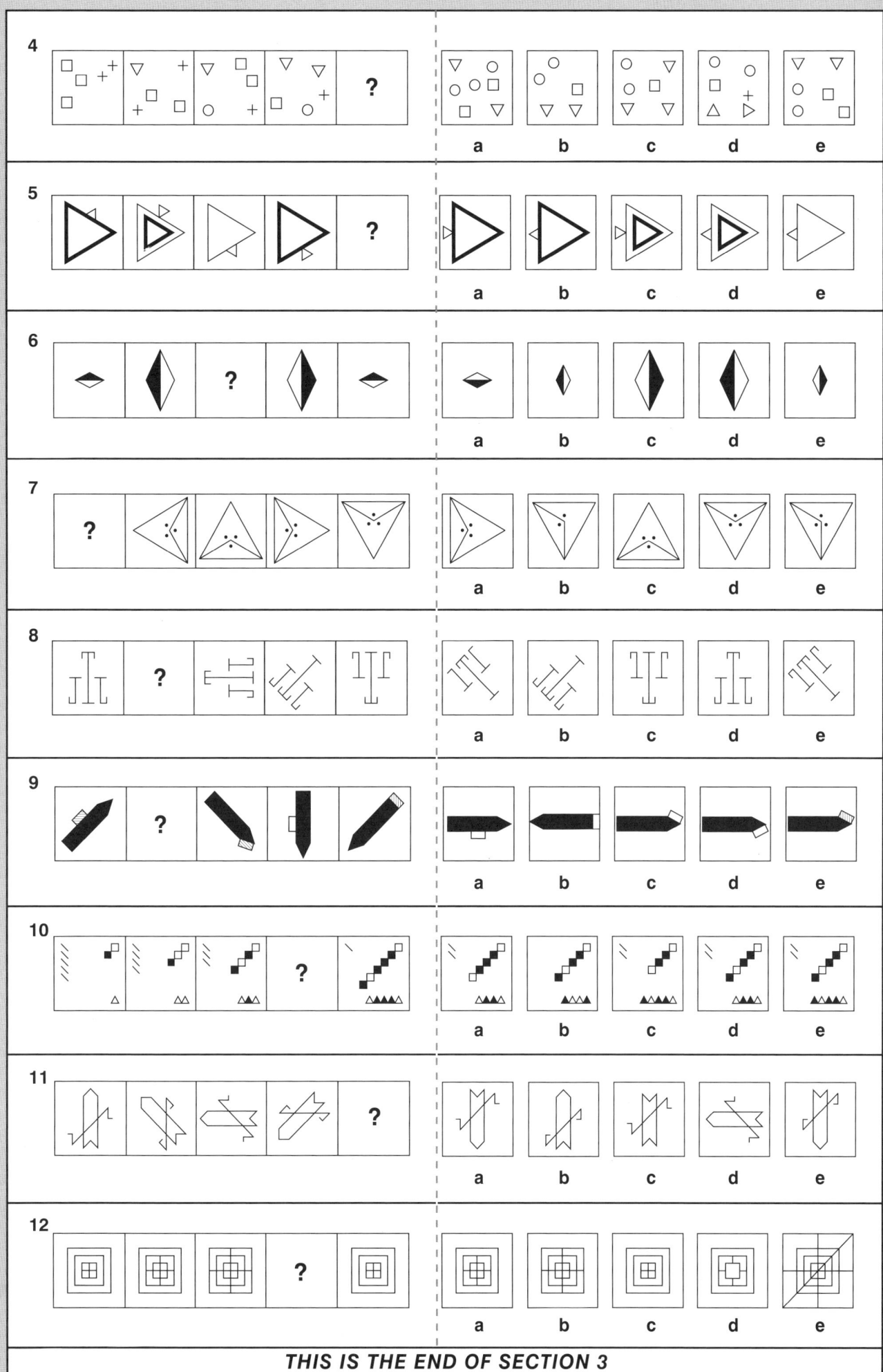

Section 4

Which code matches the shape or pattern given at the end of each line?

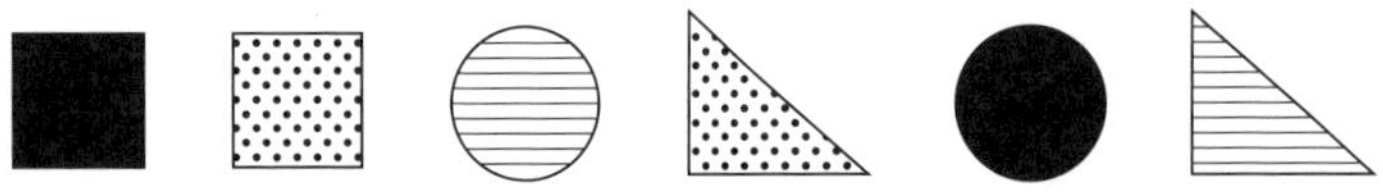

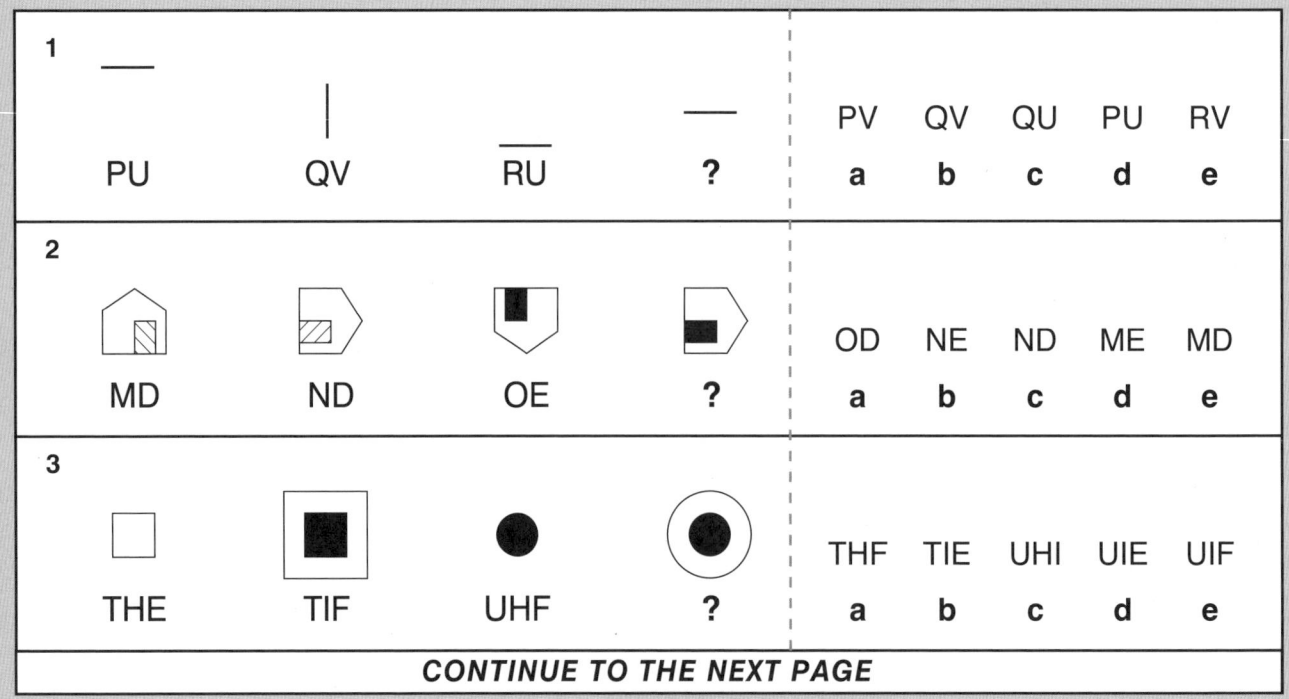

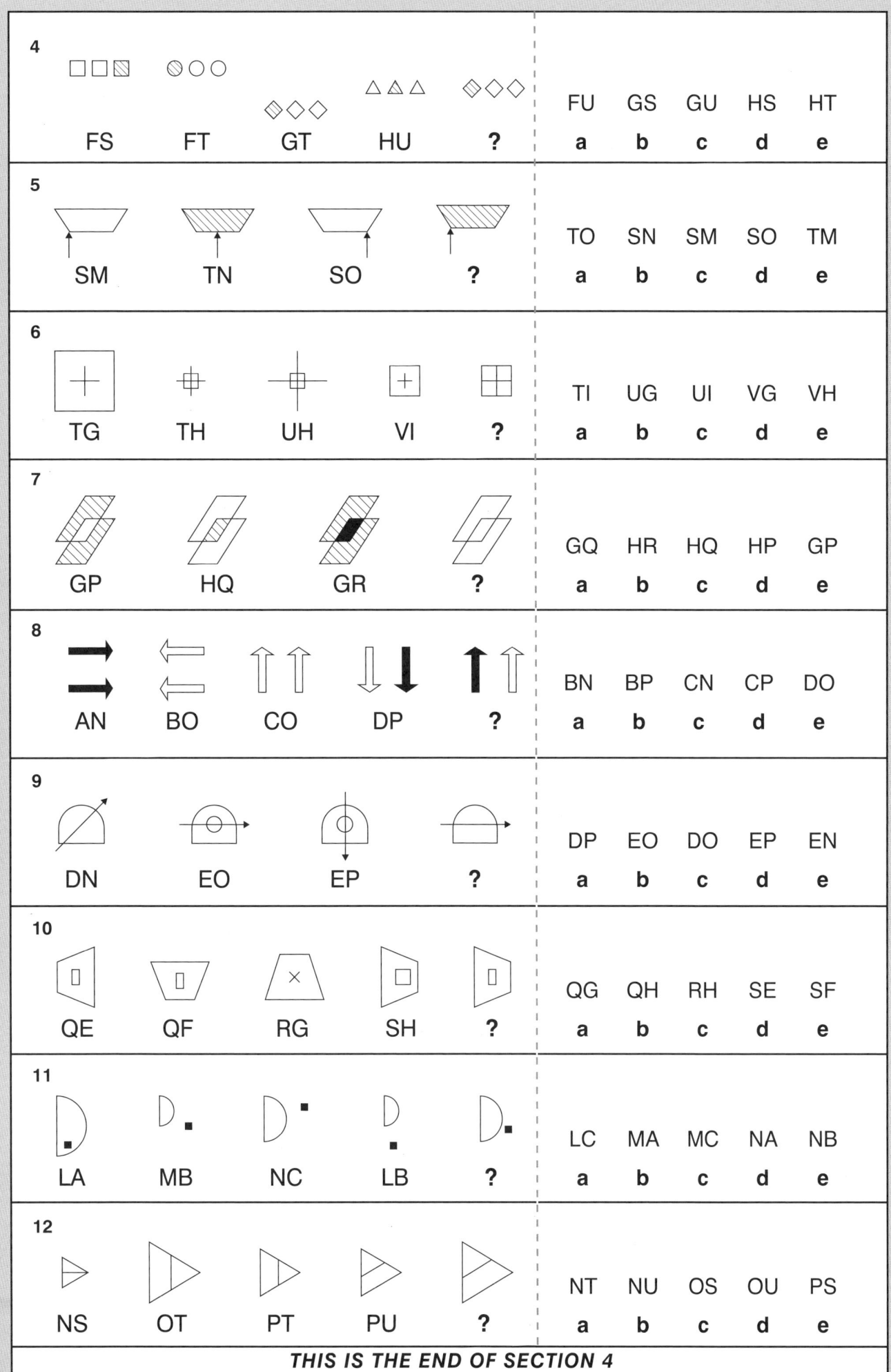

Section 5

Which shape or pattern completes the larger square?

Example

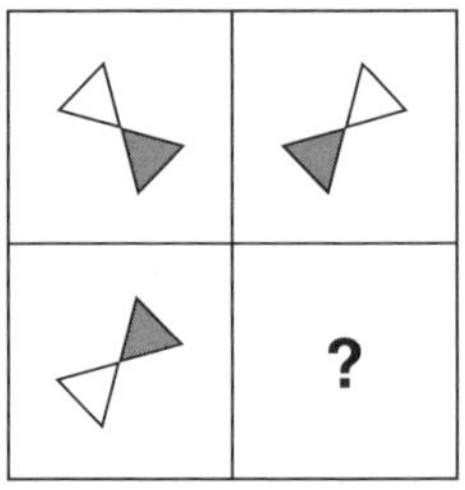

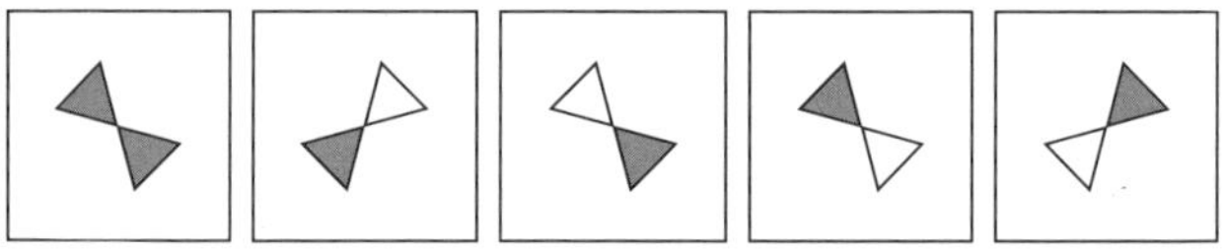

a b c **d** e

Practice 1

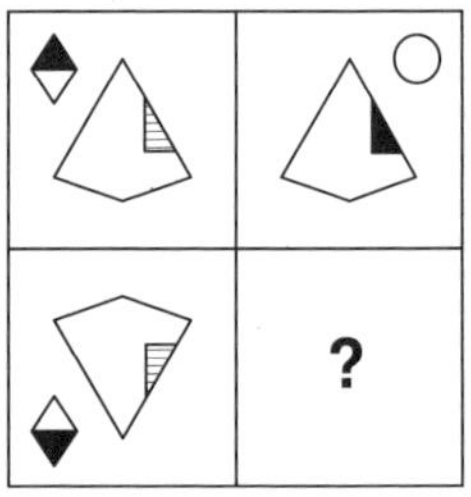

a b c d e

Practice 2

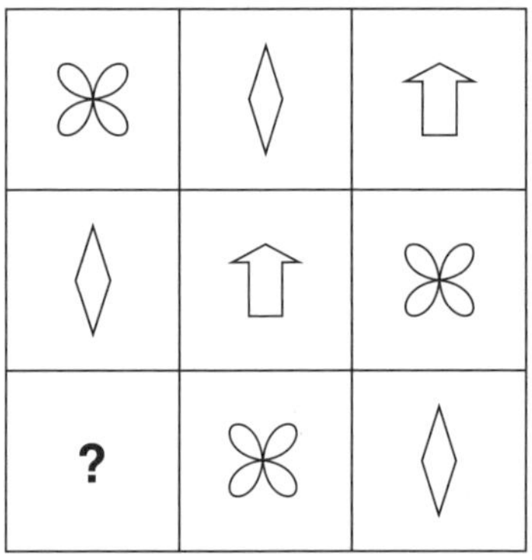

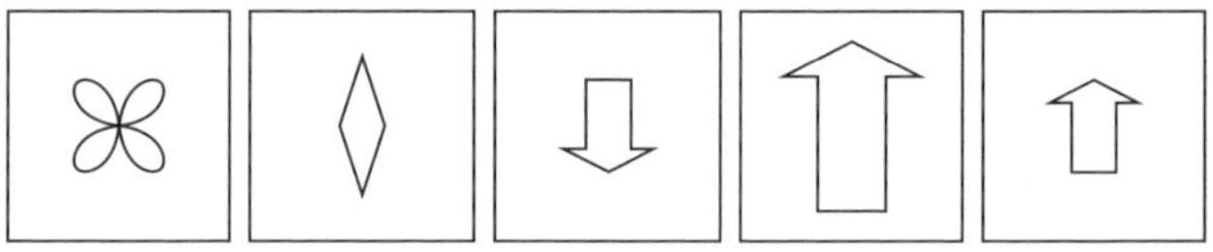

a b c d e

YOU NOW HAVE SIX MINUTES TO COMPLETE THE REST OF SECTION 5

1

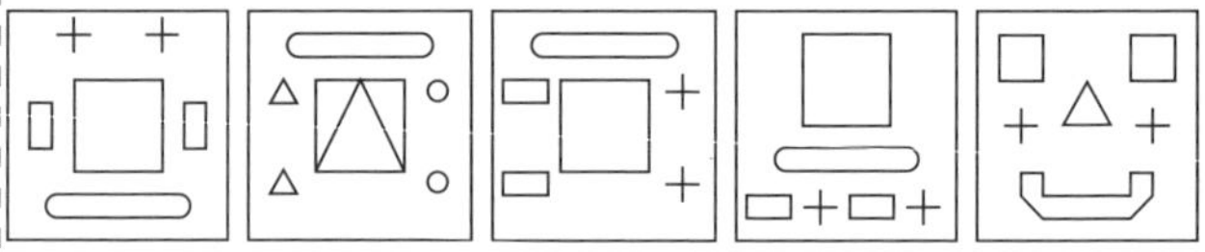

a b c d e

2

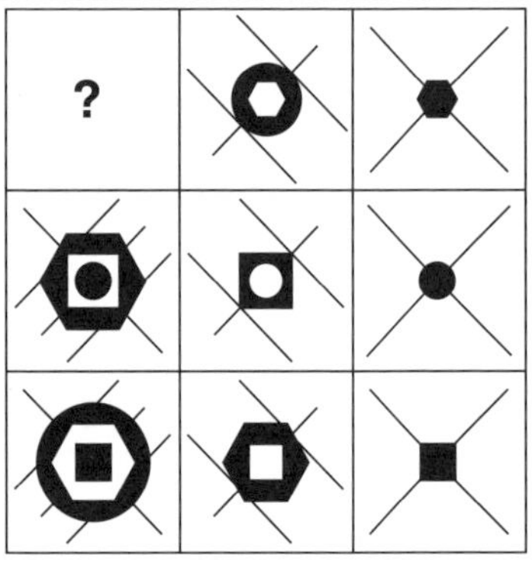

a b c d e

CONTINUE TO THE NEXT PAGE

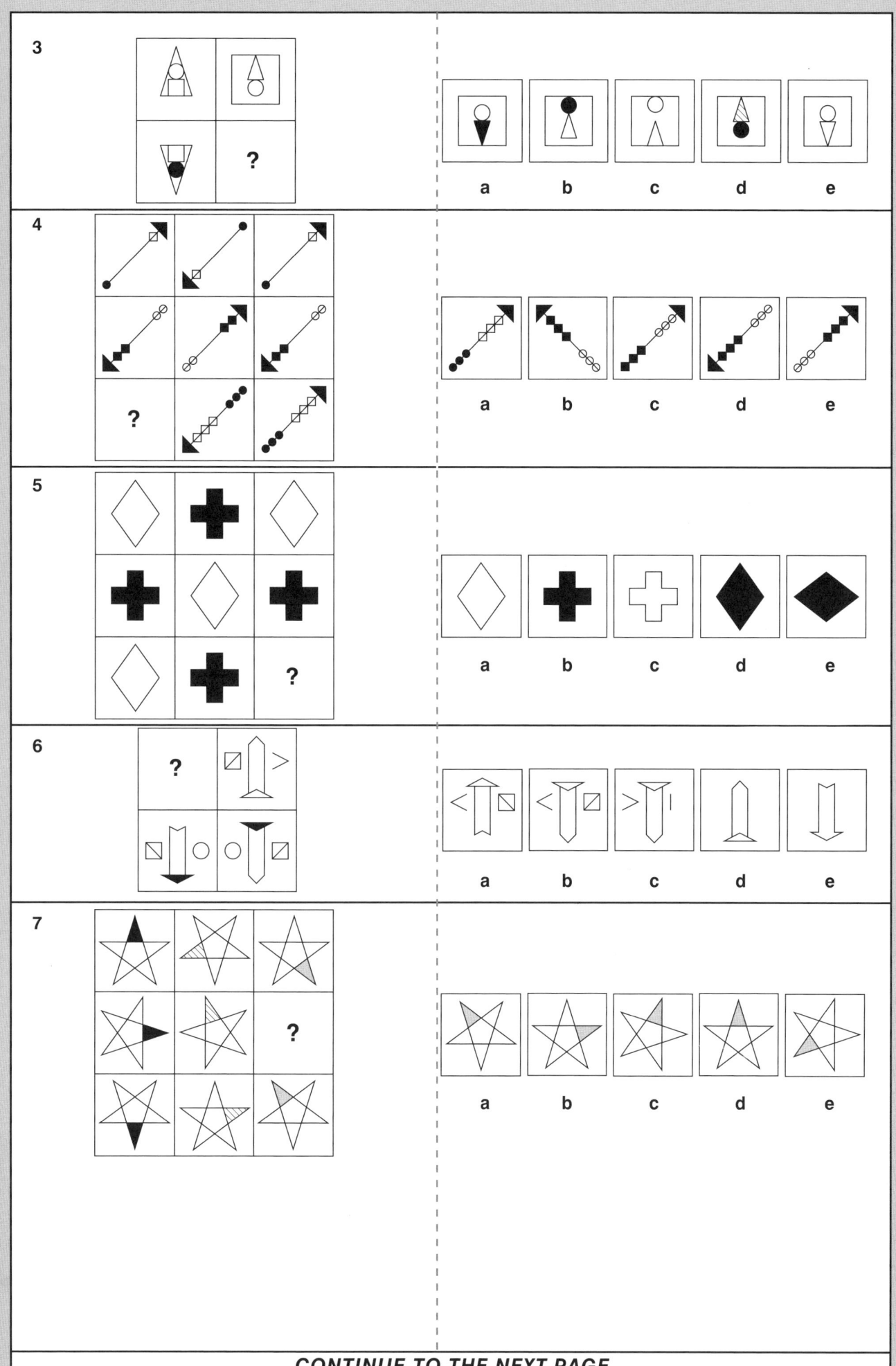

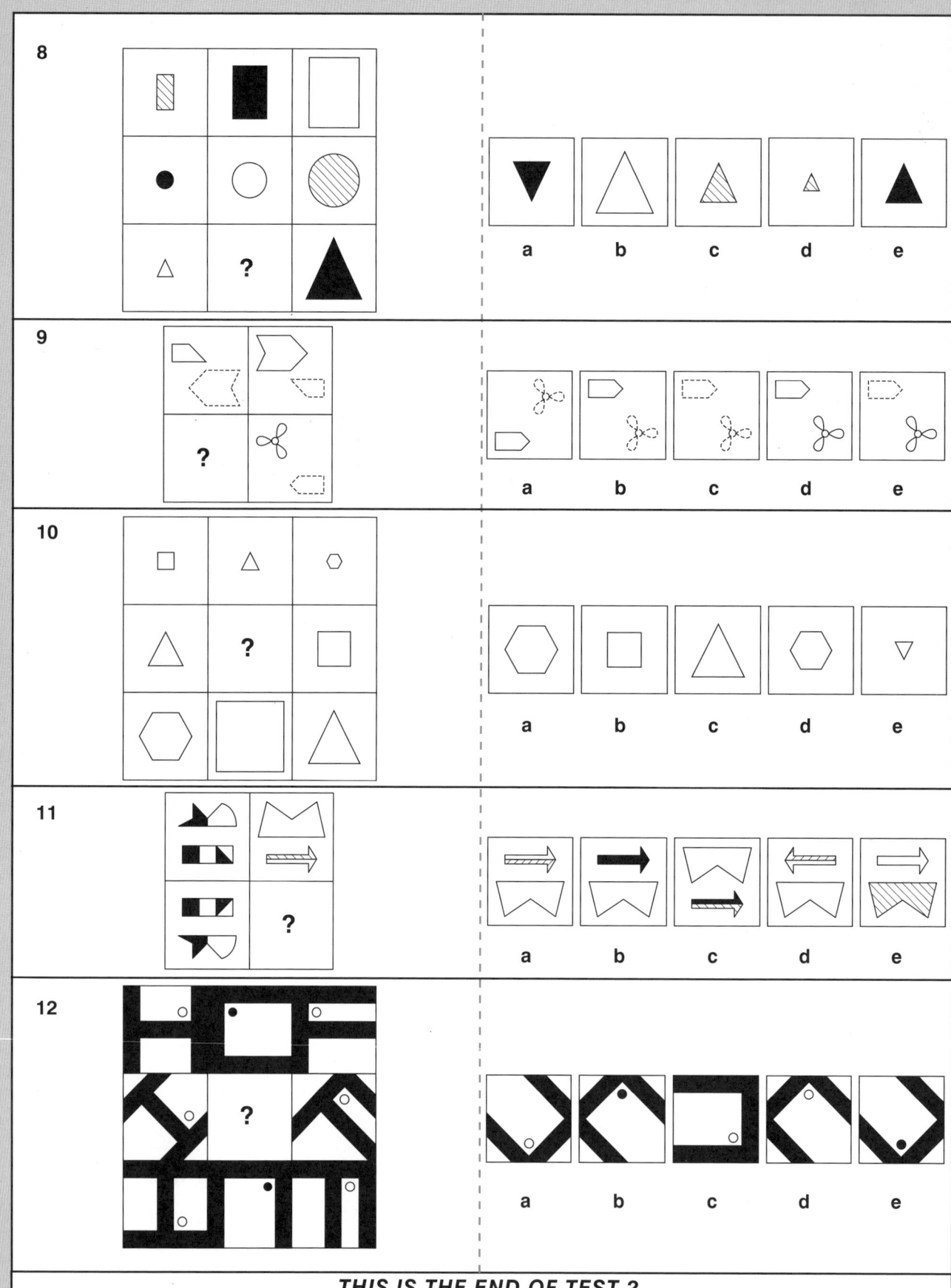